MW00325820

reclaiming our stories 2

reclaiming our stories 2

editors:
Paul (Khalid) Alexander
Manuel Paul López
Darius Spearman
Ebony Tyree

SD
CWP

SAN DIEGO
CITY WORKS
PRESS

Copyright © 2020 San Diego City Works Press

All rights reserved. The authors retain the copyrights to their own works. No part of this book may be reproduced in any form without written permission from the publisher and/or the author.

ISBN 978-0-578-52790-1
Library of Congress Control Number: 2019943562

San Diego City Works Press is a non-profit press, funded by local writers and friends of the arts, committed to the publication of fiction, poetry, creative nonfiction, and art by members of the San Diego City College community and the community at large. For more about San Diego City Works Press, please visit our website at www.cityworkspress.org.

San Diego City Works Press is extremely indebted to the American Federation of Teachers, Local 1931, without whose generous contribution and commitment to the arts this book would not be possible.

Cover design: Rondi Vasquez
Cover photo: Ebony Lee
Production editor: Will Dalrymple | Layout & Editing | willdalrymple.com

Published in the United States by San Diego City Works Press, California
Printed in the United States of America

table of contents

the stories

additional resources

acknowledgments

We'd like to offer our heartfelt thanks to Will Dalrymple and Rondi Vasquez for their layout and design expertise. Their patience, insights and vision helped realize this final publication. We'd also like to thank Kelly Mayhew and Jim Miller, City Works Press managing editors, for supporting this second volume of *Reclaiming Our Stories* with unwavering belief and enthusiasm. Special thanks go to Mona Alsoraimi, who spearheaded the initial Reclaiming Our Stories gatherings and played a central role in preparing the first book for publication. Big hugs to all of the former Reclaiming Our Stories workshop writers who generously offered their time and experience to mentor our newest participants. Without a doubt, immense gratitude to the incomparable Roberta Alexander. Her guidance and grace continue to be the twin catalysts for this ongoing community writing project, and we are indebted to her.

Finally, we offer a profound thanks to all of the readers and supporters of City Works Press. Without you, this volume could not be possible.

introduction

The original intention of the Pillars of the Community Reclaiming Our Stories project was to share experiences and build community through shared struggles and achievements. When the managing editors of City Works Press offered us the possibility of publishing our narratives, we decided to pursue the opportunity to bring these powerful stories to a broader audience. For our first edition, 500 books were printed initially, the usual number for a small, local non-profit press, but it soon became apparent that the stories had touched a nerve. Eventually, more than 6,000 books were published and sold! Our authors presented at various venues around San Diego and throughout California, and as far away as Harvard University. It has been used in many classrooms in a variety of disciplines—English, Black and Chicano studies, sociology, and others. The unexpected success of our first volume has led us to the book you are holding in your hands right now.

You are about to read the second collection of stories by our Southeast San Diego neighbors and friends. Many are, or have been, students at San Diego City College; some have completed their educational goals at other colleges and universities. Most, if not all, are first-generation college students. They have all survived and continue their struggle to overcome the constant challenges of being Black, Brown and poor in San Diego. These narratives deal with complex issues encompassing race, class, place, family, mental and physical health, gender, disability, and identity. Above all, however, they are stories of life, loss, and determination to thrive.

This project continues the tradition of a literature—beginning with the slave narrative—that counters hegemony and white supremacy. These stories offer a glimpse into the lives of real people in their own words; they put a human face to members of our communities who have been marginalized, labeled as criminals, and discarded by our society.

The Reclaiming Our Stories project was first launched in the summer of 2015. Initially our writers got together in a shared space at the Southeast San Diego Pillars of the Community office to write about any aspect of their lives—to brainstorm, share, make suggestions, and to support one another. A few of us served as facilitators, but the most important feedback came from the entire community of writers. Our goal was to complete the process by having gatherings where everybody read their stories to family and friends. In the months that we worked together, we built a trusting community of writers, and by finally reading their stories to an audience, most of our writers recognized and expressed that the experience had in many ways been both cathartic and healing.

Some of you will recognize these experiences and have lived them; others of you will learn about an aspect of life that you have not known. Each of our writers has participated in the process in a different way. Some sat down at our first gathering and cranked out their entire story. Others were not ready to face elements of their past, let alone write about them.

The authors took great risks in sharing their personal narratives. Although it wasn't the intention of the project, most authors chose to write about some of the most traumatic events in their lives. These are often honest reflections of ugly and painful realities that our authors have dealt with, often from a young age—the human stories of the consequences of systemic racism, as well as the consequences of a society in which we do not all have equal opportunity to thrive. These are stories of children who have suffered incredible trauma, who are not helped; of young people who have drowned their pain through the abuse of alcohol and drugs; of those who grew up in environments where the only role models were gang members and hustlers; of a criminal "justice" system that has "[m]ore African Americans in prison, jail, on probation or parole than were enslaved in 1850, before the Civil War began";[1] of homelessness; of immigrant families torn asunder by unfair immigration practices; of broken families; of neighborhoods where gangs and violence are commonplace.

In the back of this book, we have included journal prompts, as well as a list of related books, articles, and films that are especially useful for classrooms. These questions provide opportunities for personal connections and critical reflections. Please take a look at these features.

It is our hope that you will gain new insight into the lives of members of our community, as told through their own words.

Paul (Khalid) Alexander
Manuel Paul López
Darius Spearman
Ebony Tyree

---

1 See Michelle Alexander's *The New Jim Crow: Mass Incarceration in the Age of Colorblindness* (New York: The New Press, 2011), p. 175.

Pillars of the Community and Reclaiming Our Stories
by Pillars founder, Paul (Khalid) Alexander

Pillars of the Community began with a few Muslims and an intention to build a support system for people returning home to Southeast San Diego after incarceration. The idea was to help build a community focused on "pushing positivity" and dedicated to building a better future. Southeast has one of the highest incarceration rates in the county and has long suffered from neglect at the hands of politicians and large non-profit organizations. We recognized that in order to build this community, the people closest to the pain—who were typically overlooked and dismissed—must become (and often were) the "Pillars" of the community.

Since the inception of Pillars of the Community, our understanding of how to create positive change in our neighborhoods has continued to grow. We are constantly discovering systemic barriers that prevent people in Southeast, and in similar communities around the United States, from thriving. Today, most of our advocacy work is done through community building (pushing positivity) and policy work. Many of the individuals in this book have been involved in some of that policy work, and all have been involved in building community. Whether through legislation around gang documentation, speaking up at town hall meetings, or in exposing racial profiling, Pillars has slowly become an influential voice in San Diego politics.

Because of the high incarceration rate and the amount of police harassment, much of our work revolves around advocating for people negatively impacted by the criminal justice system. Whether we are aware of it or not, we are *all* negatively impacted by the criminal justice system. Many of the stories in the coming pages reflect that reality.

Reclaiming Our Stories

One of the things that anyone who lives or works in a community like Southeast San Diego realizes is how rich and diverse the culture is. That culture comes from the people who live here. They all have amazing stories. Although we interact with one another on a daily basis, we rarely have the opportunity to *really* understand where we come from and the building blocks of our lives that have led to who we are and how we view the world. The original idea of Reclaiming our Stories (ROS) was to create an environment where community members could come together to share their stories with friends and family and celebrate how amazing they were. Although many of the stories were of traumatic events in their lives, the fact that they had overcome those events was a testament to their strength and resilience.

I, and those who have had the opportunity to attend these readings, always leave feeling empowered and inspired. Our intention was not to publish a book but to create a space where people could grow together and feel safe talking about some of the most meaningful and transformative moments in their lives. Sitting in the cohorts and working with all of these amazing authors allowed me and the other facilitators to see the power of storytelling in action. In many cases, it was a process of healing for those telling the stories and those listening.

There is something about sharing our stories that enables us to become more human. It enables us to recognize our humanity reflected in the eyes of the audience, and it enables us to recognize their humanity in us. I hope that these stories impact the reader in a similar way. Although very little, if any, direction was given to the participants about who or what to write about, nearly all of these writers shared some of their most private and painful experiences. It became clear to all of those involved that those experiences, and the strength that was needed to overcome them, is what made the writers who they are today: strong, intelligent, and compassionate human beings.

In many ways, ROS is a critique of a broken society, a society with systems like incarceration, failed safety nets for the poor, and school districts that often fail our children. But it is also a celebration of our humanity and our ability to survive those systems and shape new narratives. By creating a space where these stories could be told and where our journeys can be honored, we are reclaiming a narrative that is often used to describe the poor, the "uneducated," and the formerly incarcerated. These narratives refuse to be dismissed. They demand to be seen. They are a testimony to the strength of our communities and the individuals who build them. There is an African proverb that goes, "The story of the hunt will always favor the hunter until the lion learns to tell its own story." I am honored to know each and every one of these authors and proud to consider myself a part of their "pride."

the stories

Richard Meza was born and raised in San Diego and will always call it his home.

Richard Meza

AL 6963

I dedicate the following story to my mother, Ruby Rentería, and my brothers, Erick and Edgar.

"BEEP."

This sound, among other sounds, woke me up, but it seemed to be quite loud for the early hours of the morning. "MEZA, MEZA," a voice said coming from the cell intercom.

"Hey, hey, wake up, man. They're calling you," Sapo said, who was one of my cellies.

It was June 18, 2012, and I found myself at the George Bailey Detention Facility. I was in 6 house, section B, and I shared a small cell with two other men, my homies, Sapo and Eric.

Sapo was all tatted down and had been to prison before. He was getting released in two months, and Eric had already done seven months and had five more to go. I had just been sentenced to do a five-year prison term at 85%, which meant I had to do at least 85% of five years.

"RICHARD MEZA," the voice from the cell intercom repeated as I climbed down from my bunk. I was at the very top of a three-man bunk. "Yeah, yeah." I responded.

"Get your things ready. You're going to prison today."

"Am I going to Donovan or Chino?" I asked, speaking to the little box on the wall. "Look, I really don't know where you're going, just that you're going to prison today. I don't get informed of where you're going."

"Okay, then."

"Good. Get your things ready and have your uniform on, and I'll pop your door open in a sec," the little box in the wall said. My door popped. I said bye to my cellies, and I headed out to the dayroom. There were three other inmates also going to prison that day. Wandering around, I heard my moniker called off from the bottom tier. "PLEITO!" I looked around to see who was calling, but all I saw was the usual bunch of metal tables with four seats nailed to the cement ground and two tiers full of cells, each tier with two sets of showers where everyone could see you. I continued to look for whoever had called me, but it was early, so the lights were still off in the dayroom. "PLEITO, IT'S MOSKA." Moska was as black as the night sky but identified himself as a "homie." I headed towards his cell. "Catching the chain, huh? Where you going?" he asked.

"Yeah, yeah, I don't know where I am going," I said. Catching the chain was a term used by inmates that basically meant going to state prison.

"Alright, I guess I'll see you up there then," he said.

"I'll see you again, homie, don't trip," I said. Although I never did run into him again, we talked for a bit, speaking to each other from the side of his cell door, as I was in the dayroom and he was in the cell. He had woken up early due to his cellie also going to prison that day.

The officer told us to exit the building. He made the announcement through a speakerphone in the dayroom. As I was leaving the building, Moska shouted: "Ima take the seven," referring to a deal the DA had offered him.

"Do it, foo," I responded as I headed out the building for the holding tanks.

We were locked in the holding tanks, waiting for the prison bus to pick us up. There had to be at least thirty inmates in there, most wondering which reception we were going to. One of the woods in the tank stood about six to seven feet. He stood at the tank's window and shouted, "STROLEX. YOU FUCKING STROLEX. FAGGOT ASS BITCHES" to some other inmates as they walked and lined up to go into another holding tank. Those inmates seemed different. They walked with their heads down as if they were ashamed, and none of them talked to each other. Afterwards, half of the inmates in my tank stood up and started shouting, calling them "pieces of shit, rats, chomos and fucking PCs." PC stood for "protective custody," and in the general population it was viewed as the worst thing you could be. They were viewed as child molesters and snitches. The one way to identify them was the color of their wristband, which was yellow. After that, the bus finally arrived. The bus ride was about five minutes, and our question about which prison we were heading to was answered when we ended up at Donavon for reception.

Once we arrived, we went through the usual process: we stripped down, butt-ass naked, and were given another uniform to wear. This one was orange and had black letters on the shirt and pants that read CDCR. We were then locked in another holding tank.

Lunchtime came and we got a bag with peanut butter and jelly and four pieces of bread, along with some crackers. The food seemed better than the food in County. We ate and talked and waited. I could hear another group of inmates coming, but I couldn't see them, because they were locked in the tank next to mine. Staring out my tank's window, I saw that they were let out one at a time, and some of them got to put on different clothes, real clothes. I saw another inmate come, but I couldn't see his face because his back was turned to me, but the way he walked and stood was so familiar—I had to have known him from somewhere. I had an idea of who it might be, but once he took his shirt off, I thought it couldn't have been him, because this guy was way too dark. So I turned my attention elsewhere, talking to the guy beside me. After a few minutes, I saw the inmate outside turn his body towards my direction. It caught my attention, so I turned my head, and I ended up locking eyes with my own brother. The last time I saw him, GSU (Gang Supervision Unit) had raided our pad like SWAT and took him for testing positive for meth. He waved and threw up our neighborhood sign, and I threw it up right back. I tried to communicate by flashing signs through the tank's window; then someone pointed out an open slot in the door. "CARNAL!" I said through the door's slot. He asked the CO (correctional officer) if he could talk to me for a bit, "Que onda, buey?" he said while shaking my hand through the slot.

"Damn, boy, you got dark," I said.

"Yeah, boy, that sun gonna burn you here, carnal."

We talked for a bit.

"Aye foo, just so you know, vas a estar encerrado en una celda for three months. Ahí cúidate, buey." He started to leave and said, "Ahí lo vemos, buey."

"Aye wait, where you going?" I said.

"I'm going HOME," he said.

"Ah shit, I just got here, foo," I said in a joking manner.

"Alright. I'll see you in about five years."

"Take care of Moms," I said.

He flashed our neighborhood sign again, and again I flashed right back. After hours of waiting in those tanks for R&R, I finally got my number, AL 6963, and got to go to a cell.

My brother wasn't lying. I did end up being in a cell for a few months, which was one of the worst experiences I have ever had. I sat in a small cell on lockdown 24/7 with another man for months. NO TV, NO BOOKS, POWDER TOOTHPASTE, HOT AS FUCK, NO YARD, NO CANTEEN, NO LAUNDRY, CELL FED, AND THREE-MIN-UTE SHOWERS THREE TIMES A WEEK, not to mention no fucking deodorant. I swear, after a while that cell started playing mind games with me.

◆ ◆ ◆

On July 8, 2013, a year had passed, and we had started a prisoner's statewide hunger strike, maybe the biggest hunger strike in US history. I was in Centinela, where it was really hot. We refused to eat state food and refused to work. The next morning it was all over the news: 30,000 inmates statewide and out of state protested. The purpose was to protest harsh conditions in the SHU (security housing unit). In my prison it only lasted a week. Some inmates in the SHU refused to eat for months and eventually died from it.

Around the same time, every California prisoner received a memorandum confirming that the federal courts ordered the state of California to RELEASE 10,000 inmates by December 31, 2013. A lot of inmates, including myself, thought that was actually going to happen. Then a few months afterwards we received another memorandum signed by California Governor Jerry Brown and the secretary of state saying that they were going to transfer us to a private prison out of state instead of releasing us. Being that I spent my free time in the library, I discovered that taxpayers pay about $45,000 or more a year per inmate to be housed. I remember thinking: that be a shitload of money.

By December 1st, I ended up in Florence, Arizona in a CCA (Corrections Corporation of America) prison. CCA is the biggest private prison corporation in the US, private prison meaning "for-profit" prison. These prisons profit by cutting costs wherever they can and receive as many prisoners as possible. This corporation has recently changed its brand name to Core Civic due to bad publicity.

The first thing I noticed about this place was that the cell was extremely cold, the walls would sweat, and with the AC on full blast, small icicles formed on the corners of cells—even with a uniform, sweats, and a beanie, I still couldn't sleep because of the cold. Then I noticed we got fed less food, and we weren't given access to rehabilitation or reentry programs; we barely received any school. Also, there were fewer guards here.

Six months later we were told to pack up again, and I ended up in Mississippi, about 2,000 miles away from home, San Diego. Our bus ride was horrible; we spent about two days in shackles. This place was something else: I could not understand a damn word these people said because they spoke with an accent nobody from California could understand. After a while, I just nodded my head to get them to shut up. It was obvious they were not trained. Some of them didn't do their jobs and spent time arguing with inmates about it. Most of the time they only had one staff member on duty with 120 inmates to supervise. Instead of hiring more staff, CCA just kept us in our cells for most of the day. It was worse than County, because at least in County my loved ones could visit me. There were numerous times when I saw inmates get jumped for ten to thirty minutes before staff intervened. In this prison, more people died in one year than my whole time in the California state prison. Over there, a lot of stabbings happened, but the medics and guards intervened instantly, and nobody really died. Here, there weren't any stabbings, just people dying for stupid reasons. One time four inmates died in a two-month period.

In CCA Tallahatchie County Correctional Facility, one inmate died after doing his job where he earned a few cents an hour when the guard told him to take down Christmas decorations. This guard was not trained, so he did not follow safety regulations or at least utilize his own common sense. The guard told the inmate to set a chair on top of a table, then to climb up and take down decorations. As inmates, if we don't follow the guards' instructions, we face the penalty of having to do more time, so the inmate complied. While standing up there, the chair slipped, and the inmate cracked his head open on the tile floor, which killed him. He only had about a year left and had already done over a decade incarcerated. Incidents like this are more common in private prisons than one might think, but since these BUSINESSES are so big and rich, they do a great job of covering them up. I hated being in that cell locked up for most of the day with a cellmate who was a heroin addict. That was another problem CCA did not acknowledge: these private prison guards basically risked their lives for little pay, so some of them brought drugs into the prison, selling them to inmates who then sold them to other inmates for a profit. But who really was to blame? The guards were just trying to make a living, and those inmates were trying not to starve.

CCA provided very little food to the inmate population, and I recall a time when I volunteered in the kitchen just to eat a little more. I remember one of the staff members announcing, "Cut back on the portions, we have a bigger population to feed." They always did. When I first got there, I remember there not being one single cell that was empty. That place remained filled, which made sense—the more inmates they had, the more money CCA made.

After some time, I decided to get a job in the library. While working there, I familiarized myself with laws and communicated with interesting people like Anthony Robinson Jr., who was there half the time working on his case and wrote articles about being in prison (see the New Underground Railroad Movement). He talked about how CCA was corrupt, and he talked about the warden there, Fred Figueroa. It was obvious that the warden was not from Mississippi, because he didn't have an accent and was the only Hispanic at the facility who wasn't an inmate. He wore a big belt buckle and cowboy boots. Anthony mentioned that the warden actually came from California where he started being investigated, and then went to Oklahoma where a deadly riot happened in North Fork Correctional Facility in 2011. According to inmates, a few people died in that riot. According to high-ranking employees of CCA and the media, no one was hurt in that riot, and Figueroa ended up working at Tallahatchie County Correctional Facility where I currently found myself witnessing a heroin epidemic among the inmate population. Everywhere one looked, an inmate was high on heroin. I couldn't take a shower without other inmates slamming heroin in the shower or one leaving spoons that still had heroin residue or cotton balls with blood still on them. Anthony mentioned that the warden, Fred Figueroa, was currently under investigation again. Fred Figueroa is now the warden at the Otay Mesa Detention Facility, another CCA facility (Core Civic).

We also started talking about the food, which was not nutritious and served in very small portions. Anthony had lost thirty pounds at CCA but managed to gain fifteen back. I had lost about twenty since I had been there. It seemed, on average, inmates would lose fifteen to twenty pounds. Anthony mentioned how the females would prostitute themselves; I only saw that happen once, but it still happened.

On July 27, 2014, I was walking in circles around the dayroom with my headphones. There's not much to do in CCA prisons, and for me, walking around the dayroom while listening to music was a way to get away from all the bullshit that went on in there. It was around dinnertime, and I thought I'd call home to let my mom know I was okay. For me, I really didn't enjoy calling home, knowing that the call could get quite expensive, especially in CCA, because phone time costs were ridiculous. My mom would start to worry if I didn't call every now and then, which to her, was anywhere from a week to two weeks. I wanted to call before we went back into our cells, knowing in CCA that they might not let us back out again for the night.

I picked up the pay phone and called home. "Hola, mijo, como estás?" My mom's voice answered from the other end.

"Estoy bien, ma, no más aquí." I responded. Then I heard her sobbing. My mom broke down crying, and at that moment, I already knew what had happened. When being in a cell for long periods of time, a person will start to remember everything and anticipate the way people are heading with their conversations. I mentally prepared myself for events like these when I was in Kearny Mesa Juvenile Hall before even going to County. My mom continued sobbing, "Ma, que tienes? Estás bien?" I asked.

"Tu hermano…. Acaba de cometer una estupidez," she said, sobbing.

"Pos, que hizo?"

"Acaba de matar a alguien y está en la cárcel," she said as she continued to sob: He killed someone!

I asked her to send me a copy of his discovery, so that maybe I could find some loopholes in it. I tried to comfort her with verses from the Bible.

Once I hung up, it was time to lock it back down. As I was in my cell I started thinking, damn, my brother is going to spend the rest of his life in prison. I kept remembering the last time I had seen him at Donavon R&R and how he shook my hand through the slot. Was that going to be the last time I ever got to touch my brother? Would they let me see him in prison? How was he going to handle it? Would he commit suicide as lifers do sometimes? If so, how would my mom handle it?

Then that cell starting getting to me again, and I wondered if things would have been different if my dad had been around. Would we, three sons, three brothers, have turned out differently? Would I be in prison now? I grabbed my book and started to read, since this was one of my ways to keep myself from thinking too much.

I got my brother's discovery in the mail a few months later, and once I read it, I knew my brother was going to get life for sure. There was nothing that could save him. Maybe he deserved it, I thought. Anyone who knows him would tell you he's a violent and scandalous-ass person who doesn't care about anyone but himself, and maybe not even that. I mean, he'll flip on someone in a second, especially when he's high, but he is still my brother and I love him. I didn't want to see him spend the rest of his life in prison. My brother, Erick Rentería, was sentenced to fifty-three life years in prison on June 8, 2017 at the Van Nuys courthouse. I came back to California in the late summer of 2015, and on the bus ride there we had lunch, a bag with an orange and a sandwich. That piece of orange had to be the most delicious thing I had ever tasted; after all, it had been over a year and a half since I had had one.

I was released June 19, 2016. With a different perspective, I accepted the fact that I was brainwashed as a kid, that gangbanging was a bullshit phase that was basically over by the time one turned twenty-one. Prison was even more bullshit, a bunch of snakes that came to you acting concerned, saying they're here to look out for you, then have the audacity to offer you some dope. I saw a lot of youngsters like myself turned dope fiends by people who called themselves homies or "RAZA."

If I could go back in time, I would have stayed my ass in school.

Ryan "Flaco" Rising is now a student leader at San Diego City College with a vision to end recidivism and to build the prison-to-school pipeline. Formerly incarcerated, Flaco is using his experience to help inspire change and reduce the mass incarceration epidemic that's destroying so many communities in our country. He believes that it is up to us, together as one, to create change in our communities.

Raising My Children from a Prison Phone

*I dedicate this story to all the mothers and fathers who are
incarcerated and raising their children through a prison phone.*

I raised my son and daughter through a prison phone. I would call them loyally every weekend while they were at my mother's house. I remember when my daughter was four years old, she said over the phone, "Dad, I want to have a picnic with you in the park." I almost broke down and cried; it was so painful to hear my little princess want to share a special moment with me in the park. I promised her I would be home soon to have that picnic in the park. My first son, Riley Richie Rising, was born two months after I went to prison. I remember my mom brought him down to visit me from Montana to Blythe, California where I was incarcerated in Ironwood State Prison. She spent a bunch of money on an airplane ticket and a hotel, but the day before her visit, an inmate ended up beating up a correctional officer on the yard, and the whole prison was put on lockdown. I was so heartbroken. I remember how dark I got after that day. I had a sense of anger, and this manifested into a violent mind.

I raised my son and daughter through pictures in the mail and through that state phone. They always interrupted our beautiful talks, reminding my beautiful children and myself that I was a slave in prison.

*You are talking to an inmate in the California Corrections Center.
This call is being monitored and recorded.*

This is how I had to raise my kids for the most precious moments in their lives, when they needed their father the most; that is how it was.

I remember hearing my son say "Dad" for the first time over the prison phone. I remember when I bought a secret cell phone. It cost $1,200, and the things I had to do to keep this phone were insane. I had to dig a hole in my concrete wall with a piece of metal, and before every yard I would have to put it back into that little hole and seal it back with state-issued toothpaste powder mixed with the concrete I had dug out of the wall. I had this phone for four months and bonded with my children all the time. I'll never forget the day I lost it.

The correctional officers came up to my door.

"Cuff up, Rising. Cuff up, Rising." And they cuffed me and my cellie up and put us in the shower next to our cell and locked us in. My heart was beating fast because I knew that was the end of my cell phone. I remember when they found it, they started to cheer, "Yes! We got it." My heart sunk. Then they came back to put us back in the cell, and I asked them.

"Hey, CO, why did you search my cell in the first place."

"One of your homies snitched on you," he responded,

"What's up? Tell me who it is," I asked him,

"You know I can't do that, Mr. Rising."

When me and my homie got back to the cell, it was demolished. It looked like a hurricane had hit our entire room. Everything was upside down. Top Ramen soups, coffee, and beans that we buy from the inmates' store were all over the floor. As we started to work on putting our cell back together, the CO came to our door.

"Rising, cuff up. We're taking you to the hole." I was in the hole for conspiracy to deal drugs. It was isolated, dark, very alone, very quiet, just you and your thoughts, and my thoughts were, "Who was it? Who snitched on me?" One of my homies said I was the main drug dealer of the block, which was a lie. I sat in the hole for 30 days until they released me back in the yard. Alone, angry, pissed, broken, and feeling betrayed. I remember when they let me back out to the yard, they put me in the same cell with my cellie, which was cool. I told him what had happened, why they took me, showed him my paperwork. After that, I didn't trust anybody. Who could I trust? Someone was looking in my eyes and then turned around and was telling these correctional officers bullcrap behind my back. I remember when I got to talk to my kids for the first time after being in the hole. It felt amazing to talk to them and hear their voices; it soothed my mind and reminded me that I was going home someday soon. But that lady came in:

You are talking to an inmate in a California correctional facility.
This call is being monitored by a recording.

I had to hear that recording five times in fifteen minutes. How am I supposed to raise my children like this? What is this teaching them? Is this really what it's supposed to be about?

I raised my kids on this phone until they released me seven years later. I had never even seen my son 'cause the one time my mom made all that effort to bring him to me, I was on lockdown.

You have sixty seconds remaining on this recorded phone call.

Then I got out. The gates opened up at New Folsom State Prison, and I walked out of the devil's playground alive. I didn't get to see my kids right away. We were still talking over the phone and through video chats, but there was no recording. Then the day finally arrived. I got to go meet my kids for the first time in my son's life, and my daughter hadn't seen me since she was a year and a half. This day was amazing for them and myself. I went to their school, met their teachers, and did a parent-teacher conference. For the first time in their life, I got to do what a father should do, and that's be involved in their life. After I met their teachers, I finally got to meet my kids. I remember my son walked in the door. He looked at everyone in the room, and as soon as his eyes locked into my soul, he screamed loud and proud, "DADDY!" He ran at full speed and jumped into my arms, pulled me to the ground, and we both started to cry. This was the first time I had ever seen my son in person. As I looked him in his eyes and studied his features, I said, "You look just like me."

He said, "Yeah," and couldn't stop looking at me, and then we hugged and I gave my son a kiss for the first time in his life. This very moment changed me as a man forever. Now it was time to go meet my daughter. They said, "Let's call her to the office." She came walking down the hallway, and her brother said, "We got a surprise for you." As soon as she looked me in the eyes, my heart skipped a beat. She threw down her backpack and ran at full speed, yelling at the top of her lungs, "DADDY!" It had been seven years since I had seen her. Then, she had been a little baby walking around. Now, she was grown and beautiful. Her brother said, "Come on, cry." But she was so strong and we started our journey.

I was now able to call and talk to my children all the time. I got to bond with them better and call them all day. This was a huge part to our relationship, and I was never interrupted ever again by that disrespectful, degrading recording reminding me and my children that I was a slave in the California Department of Corrections. What kind of message are they sending to our children?

You are talking to an inmate in the California Corrections Center. This call is being monitored and recorded.

Cierra Robinson has been able to turn her trauma into triumph through the gift of higher education. Education essentially saved her life and allowed her to become a first-year college student, social justice advocate, and a budding leader in the community. She credits her faith and belief in herself for her ability to overcome the many challenges in her life.

Cierra Robinson

To Give Myself a Chance

I dedicate my story to all the women lifers in a California state prison who told me to keep my chin up and never come back....

November 2009. "Get the fuck out the car," he tells me. He would be better off asking me to hurl myself off a high bridge into shallow water. I feel my entire body sink into the car seat as a wave of nerves hits me so tough that it paralyzes me from the waist down. I feel my heartbeat thumping in the lower half of my throat. In my mind, I'm quietly praying that my seatbelt is jammed so that it allows me to remain in my safety position. My pimp and I are parked in a dark alley. The car is idle as I contemplate my next move. His eyes burn a hole through my black dress as I struggle to buy time in hopes that he will change his mind about me working the street tonight. It's a cold November night in Oakland, California. That makes me a little over 3,000 miles from "home" where I grew up.

Instantly my thoughts become chaotic from the energy of my pimp staring down at me. Penetrating the side of my neck with such void and emptiness in his eyes, the weird smirk on his face makes me want to kick these heels off and run as fast as I can for as long as I can. But I can't. Mentally, my pimp controls me, and I wouldn't last two days out here by myself. Sitting in the car, my mind is saying, I can't do this. I won't do this. I'm so over this life. A redundant rant of mine that I recite for courage. I look my pimp in the face, and in a soft whisper all I can manage to say through the fear in my body is, "Please don't make me get out."

Four years I've been working for the same pimp, and it never gets any easier. He and I have gone through this same routine day in and day out. He knows all my stall tactics at this point. Brushing my wig, faking my period, pretending to lose my phone, or leaving my condoms back at the hotel room. Nothing works with him. He demands that I be ten toes down and bring him back all the money possible, no ifs, ands, or buts about it. Here I am, an adult coerced, forced, and deceived into prostitution. I was held in service through psychological manipulation and physical force by a pimp named King.

◆ ◆ ◆

February 29th, 2010 at 11:10 p.m. my life changed forever. We had just been pulled over by police for having a broken right headlight on our car. The officer took one look at us inside the car and already knew what part of the game we were in. All he had to do was prove it. I didn't know at the time, but my pimp and I were about to get locked up in Orange County for pimping and pandering after being pulled over with two other working girls in the car. I had never been so scared in my life. I was separated from everyone and everything I had ever known. I remember thinking while sitting in the car, "Jesus, please forgive me!" I can't live like this anymore! Now, I had prayed this prayer before and always wondered why God didn't hear me during my four years of being pimped. Here was the difference between then and all of the other times: This time I really meant it. I needed to be rescued and not by a man. So as the sirens rang out, and police surrounded us with car after car, I prayed to be rescued....

The criminal justice system took eleven months to find me guilty on charges that didn't fit my actions. Eleven months of 23-hour lock downs, with recreational yard once a month, no phone calls from family or friends, no visits, no commissary, and a two-month trial of me fighting my case. The prosecutors labeled me a monster to society. A danger to the community, they said, so the DA asked the judge for the maximum sentence possible. Twelve years at 85 percent, even though I had no prior arrest record. Heartbreaking stories like mine demonstrate what is broken about our current judicial system and why I personally feel committed to fixing it. Instead of treating victims of human trafficking with empathy, they are often thrown into the criminal justice system, labeled prostitutes, and left with few options but to return to a nightmare lifestyle that shockingly still exists in the United States.

That night we got pulled over, I honestly thought that the police would step in and help me. Save me. Rescue a black girl like myself. Get me out of harm's way. In fact, I expected them to shield all the girls in the car that night. After all, we were just lost girls who had strayed too far from home. Honestly, I felt as if the police were about to protect us from the evils of street life. The blue and red light danced across the night sky, filtering into the inside of our tinted black-on-black Mercedes Benz. Through blank stares and tired eyes, I tried to communicate to the other girls in the car that everything would be okay, and that the police would safeguard us from the beatings, the starving, the prostitution, the fear of having to risk our lives for fast cash. I finally saw a light at the end of the tunnel. I thought to myself that I could finally have the chance to go home now.

Instead, the court labeled me a gangbanging LA Crip pimp. Said that I was guilty by association and guilty of aiding and abetting. On my sentencing day at court, they stripped me of what little humanity I still had, and that left me speechless. My 56-year-old father was present in the courtroom as my only support system at the time. He stood three feet behind me and painfully watched the system fail me. The court didn't care about the trauma I had endured. They didn't care that I myself was a victim of human trafficking. Nor did they care how this would affect my family, who were left to pick up the pieces of my shattered life. All the court wanted was a conviction. Once again, I would be held captive in my life. This time by CDCR, the California Department of Corrections and (supposedly) Rehabilitation.

Right before I got out of prison, I thought to myself, How would I face my family and friends? Who was I, and what had I become? How would I ever have a real existence? A real family, a real job, a home? I took a moment to flash back to how I had ended up in this situation in the first place. I was lured off Facebook by King who promised me the world. He sold me a dream of living a life of prosperity and pretended to be my boyfriend until the day he told me, if I loved him, I would make money in this lifestyle to support us until that dream came true. He had used a tactic on me called boyfriend/girlfriend pimping. You see, I was lured into prostitution because my pimp pretended to love me, and this is how young girls like me get caught up in the lifestyle, and the Internet was just another avenue used to find and prey on girls.

On my departure day from prison, I was just a prostitute felon according to the state of California, and with that thought in mind I paroled with tears and mascara running down my face. I remember at the gate the lifer that had taken me under her wing. My prison mother, A.K.A. Mommy Mae, told me that the reason she had taken a liking to me was because I reminded her of her daughter back home. The reason she protected me on the yard was because it gave her a sense of nurturing that she couldn't place onto her blood-born child. A child that was currently being pimped, controlled by a man that was well on his way to running her into the ground. "Never come back behind these walls, Cierra; you're not made for the prison life." So, alone at the bus station, I wrote a letter to God—my tears smeared on the pages. And yet I felt somewhere far away that God was trying to pull away the cobwebs of my damaged soul and bring me back to life. It was then that my journey became so much deeper than just the desperation for my freedom from prison walls. I decided to take a leap of faith and begin to heal from all the pain, the disappointments, the lies, the shame...all of the guilt! And guess what? I never turned back. I never went back to that lifestyle or put myself in a position to be lured back into that life again. I finally found my truth right here in San Diego, California, and it wasn't in some man, materialistic objects, drugs, or a fantasy world. I found it in my ability to have faith and give myself a chance.

Asma Abdi was born and raised in San Diego, as a daughter of refugees who immigrated from Somalia. She is now an undergraduate student at UCSD.

Asma Abdi

I Swallowed My Voice

*I dedicate this story to my younger self and all who have been
silenced and intimidated by those in positions of power.*

Some details have been changed to protect the privacy of certain individuals.

I was born and raised in San Diego, the daughter of refugees who immigrated from Somalia. I may not be as American as apple pie, but I have never left this country, and I am proud to say that the United States is my home. So in my last semester of high school, I was surprised to face something that was far from what I had anticipated.

I was 17 when my teacher called me Osama. Quickly he excused himself, blaming his so-called dyslexia. I brushed it off until it happened again, a couple days later. He was working on a math problem on the board when he looked at me and said:

"So what do I do next, Osama?" I was confused and turned around just to realize he was speaking to me.

He then said, "Oh, I said Osama, I meant Asthma," and started laughing as the class joined him in a roll of laughter. It was not funny at all. I was hurt because people were really finding humor in this. His comments triggered painful elementary school memories of kids bullying me, making fun of my name, and pulling off my little hijab. I felt so little at that moment. I heard faint comments from the other students.

"You look pissed off."

"That was so racist."

"Are you okay?"

No, I wasn't okay. I felt very offended. In the Quran my name means high, exalted, great, but in that moment, I had never felt so low. The teacher moved on but had the nerve to keep telling me, "Focus." How could I focus? You mean forget? I just kept thinking how could this be happening? In my high school classroom? In 2015? I was shocked and completely disconnected. Feeling extremely bothered I gathered up the nerve to talk to him directly the next day right after class. He gave me a fake-ass apology while referring to my hijab as a "head thing." There's a lot of power behind those words, especially coming from a teacher.

Weeks later in class, the same man was speaking about his former time in the military and about the war in Iraq. He began asserting that women in the Middle East "aren't allowed to learn, go out, or do anything without approval or permission." Then he walked towards me, saying, "For example, I can come up to her and rape her without warning, and she wouldn't be able to do anything about it." Pointing at another American Muslim woman of Somali descent, he said, "And she'd probably end up in an arranged marriage." Our rowdy class became more silent than it ever had. As I sat there stifled, nobody said a word. I swallowed my voice, my eyes began to well up with tears, and I ran out of the classroom.

That cold silence that followed the teacher's violent words along with feelings of isolation kept replaying in my mind. Not only did he treat us like show-and-tell items, he didn't even know the difference between the Horn of Africa and the Middle East! I didn't know what to do. I thought maybe there was nothing I could do. Still I knew what had happened was wrong; it was difficult to dismiss his bigotry, yet I felt helpless. I didn't feel like I was capable of doing anything, but I knew nobody should feel the way I felt in that classroom.

Confused, I told my parents about what had happened. I remember my dad being infuriated that a teacher would allude to rape like that. He said he would go to the school himself, but I insisted he didn't, and I would take care of the situation. When I told my mom, she was shocked but said, "Iska dhaaf," which is Somali for "let it go"; however, she never stopped insisting on me switching schools. Although I didn't agree, I understood where she was coming from. They had sacrificed so much to protect me, and I had always been protective of my parents. Like so many refugees, they have often silenced themselves and ignored plenty in order to be accepted. That's the unfortunate reality for many immigrant families, leaving them fearful of challenging authority.

One of my favorite librarians at the time heard about what had happened and told me that my parents could possibly file a complaint. I didn't even know that was a thing I could do, but it felt like the right thing to do. I was really scared and reluctant, though. It was not an easy decision for us, but after much contemplation and speaking to some supportive people, we felt empowered to do it. Our librarian went above and beyond by pointing us to the proper resources and connecting us with people who helped immensely in our complaint process. I felt confident to continue with the support of my parents and those people right by my side, constantly checking up on me. With their advice I was prepared to hold that math teacher accountable for his inappropriate words, making sure that something was done about this wrongdoing.

Eventually we met with my grade-level counselor to mediate the issue, but nothing said explained the teacher's actions adequately. In fact, he defended himself saying that he likes "to talk about touchy subjects to relate math to freedom." What? That did not entitle him to point me out the way he did! It made so many students uncomfortable. Did he not realize the weight of his words? They were wrong on so many levels. So we filed a complaint showing how this situation and everything leading up to it had violated my guaranteed Student Rights: "to be free from acts of intimidation and harassment" as stated in school board policies.

We had additional meetings with various administrators like the vice principal who all believed a simple apology would suffice. They decided to neglect the case, and for months I didn't receive a response.

I couldn't believe that not only was there no formal action being taken by the administration, but they also failed to communicate with my parents and me. Eventually, they asked me what I wanted them to do. I told them I wasn't in a position to offer them what I *wanted* to be done but that there *should* be consequences for the violation of student rights that involves harassment, discrimination, bullying, and intimidation. After weeks of no response, the vice-principal investigating the case finally left my parents a voicemail stating that he was writing a report and couldn't share the details but that we could "file a more formal complaint." But then he added, "I will tell you that, umm, it is hard for me to see how this is really intentionally discriminating against any particular group." I was disappointed but not surprised. These issues carried serious consequences, and the school was doing absolutely nothing to prevent further incidents like mine from happening. Instead, at the next meeting, I was offered psychological counseling.

I was over it. It felt as though nothing would come out of this and I was wasting my time. I was ready to drop the case. What stopped me was the support I was receiving. This wasn't just my case: I had my parents, teachers and students fighting by my side. With their assistance I got into contact with an attorney at the Council on American Islamic Relations (CAIR), who was so helpful in holding those administrators responsible. My attorney wrote a legal notice to the school representing me. In her formal notice, she demanded the school take action to resolve any and all disputes regarding my case. In it, she explained the school's failure under the law, eloquently stating how it was a case involving both sexual and religious discrimination, and the multiple California codes. She also described the pattern of bigoted statements by the teacher and the school's attempt to intimidate me from making allegations. She told me, "Let's give them a healthy three weeks to respond." But let me tell you, the next morning the vice-principal was looking for me everywhere! She showed up to our final class potluck, but I wasn't there. Suddenly she felt the urge to speak to me. Interesting. It wasn't until the end of the semester, when the campus was threatened with a potential lawsuit for violating state laws, that they took action. That math teacher stopped working for a while and had to take special training classes. All along, he's the one that needed counseling.

This was the first time I experienced this type of bigotry and spoke up against it. Doing so has strengthened me. At the time I felt threatened, and it was difficult to wrap my head around everything that was happening. My victory may not keep more instances like this from happening in the future, but it has taught me that when people in positions of power do the wrong thing or disrespect us students, they ought to be challenged. In the process, I found my voice.

Graciela is the proud daughter of immigrant farmworkers from the Central Valley with dreams of changing the world.

Graciela Uriarte
The American Dream, Part II

*I would like to dedicate this story to mi Apá, Amá, sisters, Mama
Delma Graciela López, and my UCSD family.*

On my first day of college, my superhero had his superpowers stripped
away right before my eyes, and there was nothing I could do to help him.

Describing the scene:
It was 5:30 a.m. on a warm August Sunday morning in Tijuana, Baja
California. I had hardly slept from the anticipation, excitement, and
anxiety about my first day at UC San Diego. My dad and I had driven
down from Mendota two days prior to spend time with my grandmother
who lives in TJ. Our longtime family friend, Pechocho, was with us. He
is a 63-year-old day laborer from LA who had taken my dad under his
wing when my grandpa passed in 1995. The entire weekend I could sense
my dad's energy, a mixture of pride, nervousness, and sadness. Maybe
because he was dropping off his first daughter at a university he knew
nothing about, six hours away from home.

That morning from a distance we could see the crowded cars stretch-
ing out at least four miles, signaling to us that we would be waiting a
minimum of two hours before crossing the border. In the two hours of
waiting in line, I had to mentally prepare myself to translate and explain
my dad's green card situation, as I did every time we had crossed the previous three years. You see, my dad had issues crossing with his green card
because our second cousin, who shares his first name and paternal last
name, had unfortunately got into some trouble while crossing the border

in Arizona. Since then, my dad would have me explain to the immigration officer he should not be mistaken for my cousin.

We pulled into the gate with an immigration officer who I had wrongly assumed would be friendly. She was what I presumed to be Latina; therefore, I thought that I would not have to do too much to explain our situation to her, much less worry about being intimidated by her.

I reached over toward the officer from the backseat of my dad's Ford 150 truck to hand over our documents and tried to explain in advance why my father's green card would bring a flag up in the system. I tried to explain to her that my dad was not the man who popped up on the screen as the "criminal." She did not listen.

Instead, she called for a state of emergency. This meant that in a moment's notice the entire border at the Otay Mesa port of entry was closed down: gates shut behind us, sirens went off, and it looked to me like a dozen German shepherds with their officers started running toward us. I was confused and afraid.

Then I remembered, I had to switch into my role as the interpreter. A role that I had had to get comfortable with as early as grade school. I learned to assume the important position of my parents' advocate in the doctor's office, on the phone with customer service representatives, and negotiating with pesky car salesmen.

On this day, I was responsible for explaining what was happening to my dad and Pechocho! The officer was yelling at my dad to hand over the keys to the truck and ordered us to put our hands up and in sight at all times. First, they ordered my dad to get out of the truck. As my dad opened the door, I started to think, "What is happening? Am I going to make it to UC San Diego? Why are they doing this to us? What are our rights?" Once he got out of the truck, they asked him to put his hands behind his head, walk backward toward the officers, and lastly, they asked him to get down on his knees. All the while I was painfully translating every command.

Next, they called Pechocho out of the truck as well and gave me the same commands to translate. But Pechocho had knee problems after decades of laboring in the Central Valley fields. He could not kneel when he was ordered to, and therefore he was rudely scolded for not following instructions.

I was last. They ordered me to get out of the truck, get on my knees with my hands behind my back, and kneel on the floor. I was hysterical, crying loudly through the knots in my throat, demanding that we be treated fairly. With our hands behind our backs, they lined the three of us up to walk toward secondary. I could hear immigration officers yelling, "Hoorraah!" congratulating the officers for detaining us. We were detained for hours as they rummaged through my luggage that I had neatly packed for college.

This experience is ingrained in my memory, not because of the horrific humiliation I endured but because of the powers that were momentarily stripped from my superhero.

In high school, I had worked hard. I was in the top ten of my class, involved in sports, active in the community, and maintained a part-time job. I recall the late nights in my last year of high school when it was college application season and trying to condense my motivation and inspiration to 1,250 words or less. Deep down, I knew that I wanted to convey how my father, the cotton farm worker who would work ten to twelve hours a day in 110-degree weather under the hot Central Valley heat waves, would come home to greet me with a smile and a hug. However, his hugs would ALWAYS wait until his hands were thoroughly washed because he feared contaminating me with the chemicals he was exposed to in the fields. I can vividly describe my dad's hands. They are double the size of mine, with dirt under his fingernails, permanent dark stains on his knuckles, and calluses on his palms. Those same rugged hands are the superhero hands that raised me, put clothes on my back, and food on the table. They are the same hands that played with my hair on a Chente movie night, and played volleyball over a makeshift net he had made for me when I was trying out for the team in middle school. His essence can be easily summed up to that of a gentle giant who stands at 6'1" with broad shoulders, a rugged, humble man. He is serious and stoic when necessary, but the majority of the time you can count on his happy demeanor and constant teasing that makes the sound of laughter a staple in our home.

Growing up, I was my father's consentida, his spoiled one. The daughter of Julian Uriarte López from Morelos Dos in Sonora, Mexico, an ejido, a piece of land farmed communally near Ciudad Obregón. He made his way up "North" in the 80s in pursuit of the American Dream and to follow his father, who had settled in a tiny rural California agricultural community working in the cotton farms. A lot like Morelos Dos, this city is known as Mendota, California. I was raised in Mendota from the day I was born until it was time for me to leave to pursue the American Dream, Part II. I would be the first in my family to go to college.

Eventually, we were allowed to cross the border to the American side. I made it to UC San Diego that day and went on to graduate in four years with a Bachelor of Arts in Political Science. As I write these words in 2018, my father continues to be my pillar of strength. Gracias, Apá.

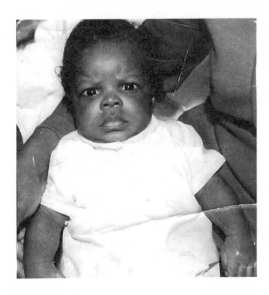

James L. Smith II is a student in the radio, television, video, and film department at San Diego City College. He has been connected to the department since 2010. He's a father and grandfather. Born and raised mostly in Detroit, Michigan, he first came to San Diego as a Marine recruit in 1981 and has been a member of the California community since.

James L. Smith II

I Hate White People

I dedicate this truth to my children, your children, and the children to come.

I hate "white people." Seriously, I do. I know it's not popular to say, but I hate "white people," not people with white skin but "white people." I grew up hating "white people." I didn't really know it at the time. Maybe it's because I lived in an environment that wasn't conducive to expressing these types of feelings for fear of retaliation, but as individual incidents happened in my life, subconsciously I began to recognize that "white people" were not good for me.

I was born "colored" in 1963. Check my birth certificate: Colored. I was born, as I believe all kids are, with no concept of racism. By the time I was six years old, my teachers and the media called me a Negro to my face. By the early 70s, I went from being colored/negro to hearing that I really was an Afro-American. This characterization was a result of perceived victories in civil rights legislation and moral equity. Power to the people! What has stuck since the mid 1600s, however, is black and nigga. Like me, black people have been searching for identity since Virginia planters stripped us of our cultural identity and relegated a mass of African cultures into a single color-based society, while simultaneously declaring themselves, and those that shared their pigment, as "white."

I'm sure many can relate. There is not a day that's gone by that "white people" haven't been an influence on my decision-making process.

I was born and raised in Detroit, Michigan, but for two years, I lived in Oakland, California. I attended first and second grades there. I had just begun to see the world outside of my grandfather's church circle. I had also just begun to make friends in kindergarten in Detroit when I found myself 2,300 miles away making new friends at a new school, E. Morris Cox Elementary. One of the cats that I met there, Tommy, came off as a real cool dude. We played tetherball, hopscotch, tag. You name it. If the game was played on a school playground, we played it, fun every day. He wasn't my only friend. There was another cat named Speedy and another cat named Eric. I remember Eric was a black dude. And Speedy was a white cat. The cool thing about Tommy was that he also lived on my way home. He was the first friend whose house I had entered outside of our apartment complex, but Tommy's mother's boyfriend made Tommy stop hanging with me because I was black. I lost my first friend because I was a little black boy. Tommy had no problems with my color, but his adult influencer did. I hate "white people."

Two years later we moved back to Detroit because my stepfather was dying of cancer. Shortly after his death, my mother and I moved into a new house that was on the deeper West Side of Detroit. Now in my neighborhood, most of the kids that I played with were black. There was one family that most would call white. They had a pretty little Indian girl that they adopted, along with a biological daughter and son. The kids played with us sometimes, and they welcomed me into their home. They may have been white but not "white people."

There were several black families around, at least eight black families that I played with. This should have been a comfortable existence, but the specter of white influence affected me even here where it was barely visible. How? Because, light was right and next to white! I believe many of these black families tried in earnest to represent what being black was about, but the influence of lesser melanin was king. The lighter your skin, the more beautiful and valuable you were considered. However, the darker your skin, the more unattractive you'd be considered. I was the darkest cat in my neighborhood, and none of them ever let me forget it.

Ironically, I never heard it from the white family, but I heard it from my perceived likeness.

"Shadow," "Black Ass," "Dot," "Night Crawler" were just a few of the debasing monikers based on the color of my skin. Shit, as much as I tried, I couldn't make myself believe that I was really an equal. I rarely ever thought that I was cute as a kid. I didn't really like black girls. I had crushes on Kristie McNichols from *Family*, Barbara Eden, Jeanie from *I Dream of Jeanie*, Marsha Brady from *The Brady Bunch*, and Farrah Fawcett from *Charlie's Angels*. There was a beautiful black girl down the street from me, Darlene. But I couldn't see that. She liked me, I found out later, but I couldn't see that. My tuner was set for brightness. Beauty, in my mind, was a "white" life. Hell, school, church, and TV said so! All I could see was that long straight hair and fair colored skin. This was my idea of beauty. My self-esteem was stunted by people who didn't look like me. I hate "white people."

My mother sent me to an all-boys Catholic school for seventh and eighth grade. In my first year there, I got into a fight because a white boy called me a "lucky nigger" for being able to go to that school. Regularly, I would have shined on this degrading comment and ignored this fool, but I had been fresh off a visit to my Afrocentric dad, and his side of the family didn't take shit from "white people." In fact, when they were pissed at something a white person had done, they went from white to "crackers!" Anyway, it wasn't much of a fight. I said, "Fuck you, honky!" And slapped him. He rushed me. We wrestled. A Jesuit at the school came over and broke it up. I was suspended for a week; him, for two days. I hate "white people."

The next year, I guess fucking with the black guy was still in vogue. Twice I came out of the gym to find my clothes in the pisser, my shirt the first time and my shoe the next time. A few days later, one of the guys that I thought had done it walked into the bathroom stall. I hurried and changed, then ran into the bathroom, pulled out my shit, and pissed over the stall onto his head. I heard him scream. Then I realized it wasn't him, and I took off. This mixed kid that ran around with the guys who fucked with me had just become the victim of my revenge. I partially felt for him, but that's what his "shade hating" ass got. Yet this Indian guy dimed me out. And that's after I paid him five dollars not to tell. This is mid-70s. Five dollars ain't no chump change for an eighth-grade black kid. My mother was called to school and they told her everything about the pissing and the bribery. My mother drove me home, pulled into the driveway, put the car in park, and then socked me in the jaw, just like Nick Nolte did to Eddie Murphy in *48 hours*. Wow! A beatdown by my mom over a white dude. But I still see him now in my memories, pee dripping off his curls—curls he got from "white people." I smile. I hate "white people."

There have been many other crucial moments in my life when "white people" have fucked me over. From my courtmartial by an all-white forum for coming to the aid of a black friend being beaten up by two white guys bigger than him, to the white dude that called me a nigger while I was in the brig serving time for the former and cost me 28 days in the hole, to the white corporal who thought so low of me to continuously poke me in my chest until I put him on the ground, sending me back to the brig. At 17, I originally bought into the idea in boot camp that there was no black and white there. We were light green or dark green Marines. Brothers above all others, and, in many ways, it was, but "white people" ruined that for me. I hate "white people."

I could tell you about the run-ins with LAPD and the multiple times that I "fit the general description." Above all, there was the time that I lay prone as instructed while they stomped my legs and rubbed my face into the cement while some asshole shot uppercuts between my legs, trying to hit me in the nuts. Meanwhile, my then eight-year-old daughter watched. I saw fear on her face as she screamed, "Daddy!" I screamed,

"MY DAUGHTER!" And only then did a sheriff move her, but the images are still with both of us to this day.

Interactions between the police and black people are an ever-present siren that deadens the ears of society. We've heard it so much that it is exhausting to get angry over it, so it's dismissed as "one of those things." You might question my association of police to hating white people. Well, the police, criminal justice system, and "white people" have done more to hold me captive—to hold me back and to hold me down—than any other group I know. Oppression and suppression by complexion. I hate "white people."

To those of you that call yourselves white, your ancestors were not members of a white race before the 1600s. Most European immigrants and their descendants took on the race designation of "white" to enjoy, collectively and inherently, a freedom not afforded to the African or other peoples of color. In order to escape the threat of an overwhelming populace of the indentured servant/slave workforce, a class of people was created to dictate for ALL who bore the color that one race was superior to all. White. And another would be committed to servitude for an eternity. Black. I hate "white people."

Get rid of "white people" and the world can be a better place!

The final anecdote took place on campus. With it, I hope you gain a better understanding of my declaration. In 2010, I enrolled at San Diego City College and joined the radio, television, video, and film department. I tutor and mentor, for free, and have done so since I've been here. I love the vocation and enjoy helping the students find their voice and work on the skills they will need to make a career in this field, but an asshole, a "white people" sort of guy, poisoned my experience. I came in early one morning and found that the edit bays down the hall from the radio station, Jazz88, had been vandalized and some equipment was missing. I reported it to the DJ on duty, who in turn reported it to the head engineer. I was feeling for them. Seriously, I was hella upset 'cause I loved using that edit suite, but later in the day, while I was in that same suite, I heard voices. I recognized my name. So I listened.

"James and his son were here late last night. They were the last ones here."

What the fuck? But before I could get around the corner to say something, a professor in our department vehemently defended me and my son. "They weren't the last ones here last night. I was. I saw them when they left an hour before I left, and nothing was missing or vandalized when I left!"

The engineer continued to try to vilify me and mine. This was a guy I spoke to almost every day. I treated him with respect. I figured he sometimes was just a little grumpy. But I didn't want to attach any racial overtone to his personality. Though, of course, I did suspect. For this guy to point out me and my son as possible suspects in this theft, when I was the one that discovered everything, began to threaten my safety and existence at this school. An investigation gone wrong, and it happens, could have caused me to lose my kids and limit my son's future possibilities. Even if not convicted, arrests are still on your record. Yet someone who has white skin, that I don't consider to be "white people," spoke truth to foulness. I will always have respect and admiration for that professor for standing up for me and my son. It wasn't a show for me. He didn't know that I was on the other side of the wall. Shout out to Professor Bob Sly for being a righteous person.

The point is that this man, this engineer, felt so little of me as to throw me and my son under the bus for no other reason than the idea that he could (that's some real "white people shit"). For the next couple of years, I dealt with this cat, never caving into my desire to blast off on this fool. But as the saying goes, "God don't like ugly!" Later, that very same engineer was arrested and convicted for stealing cameras and gear from the department's coffers. Equipment turned up in pawnshops all across the county dating back ten years, and this muthafucka tried to put that on me and my son. Do I need to say it again? I don't hate "white people" for the color of their skin. My first-born son's mother would be considered white, though I never thought of her as that. My brother from another mother, Alex, by eyesight would fall into this category. My friends Misasi and Whitebread resembled the description, but I don't consider them "white people." Those kids, Tommy and Speedy, at the time I knew them they weren't "white people" to me. No. I hate "white people" because I went through life unknowingly hating myself while trying not to hate you.

As I see it, the term "white supremacist" is redundant. Identifying as "white" alone is a declaration of supremacy. Anyone who calls himself "white" as a race, dons the cloak of the privileged oppressor. It's simple. If "white people" don't believe in inequity based on color, then don't be "white." As I reclaim my story, I am certain that my hatred would dissipate if "white people" would reclaim theirs.

Romelia "Meme" Turner is a native San Diegan raised in Southeast. She is very active in her community with organizations such as Pillars of the Community, and she proudly serves in the usher and women's ministries at Greater Life Baptist Church. Currently Romelia is a City College student, a Promise Scholar, an Umoja Mentor, and on the Dean's list for her 4.0. She is working on her AA in Psychology with a focus on Mental Health and Black Studies.

Romelia Turner

The Fight for My Life

I would like to dedicate this story to my dad, Robert Lee Turner Sr. (1936–2008). You are my personal angel that I know as Daddy. Thank you for being an example of what a real man, husband, and father looks like, and for every lesson you ever taught me that made me the woman I am today. You are forever in my heart. I love you, Daddy. Your begotten daughter, Meme.

The Discovery

One morning in April 2008, I woke up and did a self–breast exam before getting out of bed to get ready for work at Supercuts in Del Mar where I lived. I was exhausted because I had taken on another job at Wal-Mart in Clairemont Mesa stocking in the pharmacy until two in the morning. That's when I felt something there in my left breast. It felt like a lump in the tissue about the size of the little bouncy ball that came with the game of jacks (you all remember that game, right?) I had size DDD breasts, and this lump sat right on the top left side, right where you put your hand over your heart for the Pledge of Allegiance. It was nothing that you could see; it was only something I could feel. I ignored it because I just thought maybe it would go away. I thought to myself, "My dad is fighting esophageal cancer right now, and I just know that cancer can't be happening to me, too!" My family and I were already going through a lot with my dad, so I never mentioned it. Nobody knew.

This is my story; it's a part of my life that pretty much defines who I am, a real warrior. My Name is Romelia Turner, but everybody calls me Meme. I was born and raised in Southeast San Diego, right off 43rd and Market. We call it 4 Tray or The Tray. It means "4 The Rawest-Ass

Youngsters." All the kids on my block grew up together as family and we are all very close. I lived in the hood, and I learned how to survive at an early age. We were not a gang. We were family, and we got along with people all around town. Some of us were squares, and some of us were hustlers, and some of us were both. It didn't matter. When you came to 4 Tray, you were family.

I am the youngest and the only girl by my parents, Robert and Annie, A.K.A. Sco (I love to call her that). I have three brothers, Robert Jr., Terry, and Steve, and I can honestly say they had me a little spoiled. My husband's name is Lamar, and we have two adult children, Diondre and Da'Janae. Growing up, I had always been a little reserved. I was raised in a small church named Greater Life Baptist Church in Emerald Hills. My parents worked very hard, and the rules were firm for their only daughter. I get it now. They only wanted to protect me and wanted me to have a better life than what they had had as far as education and opportunity went. I wasn't the greatest student in school, but I got by. But by the time I got to high school, I was totally failing. I drank a lot of alcohol and smoked a lot of weed, which eventually led to harder drugs. This made me a product of my very own drug-infested environment. This behavior, too, eventually led to a teenage pregnancy and me dropping out of high school with credits equivalent to the 10th grade.

I've put my body through a lot in my life. I wish I would have realized early on that I only get one body, and I need to take special care of it. Life really happened to me in the worst way. There is so much more triumph to my story, but I am going to share a certain part of my life because it is the most meaningful to me and should be shared with the world, especially my sistahs. It could possibly save someone's beautiful life. I'm a breast cancer survivor, and this is my journey.

June Gloom

A couple of months went by after I noticed the lump, and I started to worry, so I told Lamar (my boyfriend at the time) about it, and he started to worry, too. He kept urging me to go to the doctor to get it checked out, but I just didn't want to listen. I thought to myself, "He's a man. He doesn't know what he's talking about." I totally brushed it off. So after losing my dad on June 10th, 2008 to esophageal cancer, I noticed my lump had gotten bigger, about the size of a lime, and it had started to itch! Right where the lump was, my skin had turned a little red because it was irritated. You still couldn't see the lump, but at the lump's location it felt hot to the touch. I had regularly scheduled monthly doctors' visits at my OB-GYN's office because I was dealing with a cyst on my left ovary, and my doctor, Dr. Goldstein, was monitoring the size and condition of the cyst by ultrasonogram, and I still never mentioned my breast lump to him. I just thought that it had something to do with the cyst. I was wrong. I was still working both jobs, and I really wasn't feeling well, physically and emotionally.

August came around, and I was riding on the train at the park with my sister-in-law, Dire, at my family's reunion in Oakland. I told her that I was having surgery when I got back home, because Dr. Goldstein was going to remove my ovary and do a biopsy on the cyst to make sure it wasn't cancerous. That's when I mentioned the lump to Dire. I love her so much. No one would understand that she is really like the big sister I always wanted. It was her words that got me to mention it to the doctor.

The Results

In September 2008, I had a follow-up appointment after surgery from getting my ovary removed, and Dr. Goldstein had the results from the biopsy done on my cyst. It was benign! Hallelujah! Thank you, Jesus, don't ever underestimate the power of prayer. With a sense of relief, I didn't hesitate to let my doctor know about the lump in my breast. He examined my breasts. He touched, poked and mashed them all around and then sent me to get a mammogram all in the same day. Now usually if there is a mass discovered during the mammogram, there's a follow-up appointment set to come in and have a biopsy done, and oh, to my surprise, there was not just one mass, there were two! The other one was found on the side of my left breast near my armpit. One that I totally missed. This really freaked me out because now they're no longer following protocol since they immediately sent me in for a biopsy. I was afraid that it would be painful, but it wasn't too bad. The roughest part was the wait for the results which came about a week later.

I received a phone call from Dr. Goldstein himself, who told me the cells were cancerous. There I was at my mother's house, holding the phone to my ear and staring right at my mom. I felt cold, numb, and speechless as I listened to the instructions of my doctor. When the phone call ended, I turned to my mother and told her the news. She began to cry silently, and I cried along with her. In that moment, I felt defeated. But, God, in that same moment all I could do was think about my dad, and that's where I drew my strength from. So I dried my eyes for the fight of my life. The next day I set an appointment with the surgeon that my doctor referred me to, and the next appointment available was two weeks out. By this time the lumps were the size of a grapefruit.

The Wait

After waiting about three weeks to hear back from the surgeon, I had my first appointment. He gave me information about me needing another meeting with a medical oncologist for chemo. Naturally, I grew impatient. So I contacted Dr. Goldstein's office and told the receptionist exactly what was going on and how long it was taking for them to get back to me, and that I felt that my life was not that important to them. I was really stressed and worried with two symptoms that will quickly lead to death in a time like this. She put me on hold to talk to Dr. Goldstein, and then he gave me a different referral to Sharp Outpatient Pavilion for Dr. Barone, so when I called to set an appointment, I was seen that same week. After his consultation, he walked me to see Dr. Fisher, the medical oncologist. They worked side by side, sharing waiting rooms; they worked as a team so professionally and with so much care. They were both very easy to talk to. They understood me and prepared me for what I was about to go through.

They had a lot to offer me. They recommended that I take classes for knowledge about my condition. My best friend, Kathy, my rock from that day forth, went with me to those classes. This was sometime in the beginning of November. Prior to those classes, Dr. Fisher needed blood drawn and sent me to the chemotherapy lab. Now when I got there the lab tech had a very hard time finding a vein, and I told him that the women in my family were very hard to get. Get it? I will never forget what that lab tech told me that day. He said, "We're about to kick this cancer's ass!" I remember thinking, "I hope so."

My lab results came back: very aggressive stage III breast cancer. I started chemo right away. I don't really remember much about those dark days, but I remember feeling like I had hit a wall. My hair started to fall out on December 18th, my 36th birthday, and I shaved my head. I also remember my tongue turning black, and I could always smell something horrible in the room, but no one else could smell it! Chemotherapy kills a lot of good and bad cells, so I guess that was an internal scent of my own dead cells. It was horrible. I had treatment on Wednesdays, red bags first, then white bags of a strong steroid, all totaling 22 weeks. I remember my church family would come over just to sit with me to cheer me up, and then I would be the one to uplift them. I had chemotherapy treatments from December 3rd until April 29th.

By the end of my chemo treatments, my lumps were gone! So my next step was to have my breast removed. I decided to have a double mastectomy because I had had two lumps in one breast. I was told by my doctor that there was a greater chance that I would get cancer in the other breast later on in life, so I made a conscious decision to avoid any more pain or heartache for myself and my family. My mastectomy in July was a success. I remember waking up to my family and friends and my brother on the phone calling from jail to check on me. He was the first to tell me that Michael Jackson had just died. I am his biggest fan, and I could not believe it.

My Journey Continues

After recovering from a double mastectomy, I needed radiation, and what I remember from that was a quick zap to the surfaces where my cancer lived. I went to my radiation treatments Monday through Friday for about two weeks. I was feeling great! I was CANCER FREE from head to toe, and that was the greatest gift ever! LIFE.

When I healed enough to get reconstruction about two months later, the plastic surgeon I was referred to would not do the surgery, because of my weight. I was so frustrated because this was a really big deal for me. I didn't even feel like a complete woman anymore. When people say I'm beautiful or pretty, I smile and say thank you, but I really don't feel that way. When I look in the mirror, I don't see what others see. My confidence was gone, and I felt like half of a woman, and that made me more determined to reclaim my strength. I just wanted to feel complete again and enjoy life.

Now fast forward to 2018. I've had some reconstruction, but I have a few more surgeries to go, and I feel beautiful. I am still on my journey, and I am more confident in my skin than ever before. My life is great, too. I'm 45 years old with two children. My son is 27 and my daughter is 20. My mom and all my siblings are still living and loving me. I also have great friends. I attend San Diego City College on my way to transfer to a four-year university with a degree in psychology and a mental health certificate. God and my support system play a huge role in my everyday walk of life, and I don't know where I'd be without them.

Mary Coleman moved to San Diego after earning a BA in Psychology from Emory University. After receiving an MA in English from San Diego State, she worked as a tenured English professor at San Diego City College until a debilitating stroke forced her into early retirement. Mary is in the process of writing her memoir.

Mary Coleman

Five Weeks

In memory of my mother, Gail Elaine Coleman. I will always be grateful for your love, sacrifice, and support.

Too many losses, coming way too fast without any warning or negotiation. In less than an hour, a tiny clot would become lodged in one of the blood vessels in the right side of my brain, cut off the oxygen, and cause all the brain tissue in that area to die. Less than sixty minutes is all it would take for me to go from being a busy (some would say overextended) tenured English Professor and doctoral student to a permanently disabled woman forced into a recovery process none of my education or life experience had prepared me for. It took a fraction of an hour for me to start feeling dizzy while grading papers shortly after midnight. At first I dismissed it as another bout of vertigo, which I had suffered from for the past three years. Usually, the room would spin for five to ten minutes, then stop. This time it didn't, so I stumbled to the refrigerator to get a drink of water. I tried several times, but every drink ended with me choking. Dismissing my inability to swallow as a lack of sleep, I half-stumbled to the stairs leading to my bedroom. Each time I tried to take a step, I lost my balance and had to grab the banister to keep from falling.

"Are you okay?" My mother's question interrupted my fourth attempt. "Yes," I answered. My mother would later tell me that something in my voice prompted her to get up and come check on me. She took one look at my drooping face and said, "I need to get you to the emergency room." Finally, I was worried not by my symptoms but by my mother's attempt to hide her own agitation. She kept repeating things that never fully made it to the part of my brain that generates meaning. Only her tone, which said something was really wrong, penetrated.

Before I knew it, an ambulance was taking me to Tri-City's emergency room. My mother sat beside me, listening to the answers I gave the paramedics. Then I was lying on a gurney while doctors poked and prodded, asking me questions that only confused me. In the middle of all this, I heard my father's voice. My mother had called him, and he had come right away. Something was really, really wrong.

I began to pray silently, "Please God. I'm only 39. I don't want to die."

"Miss Coleman. Can you feel me poking your toes? It's going to be a little prick. Just tell me when you feel it."

"What?" I stopped praying to focus on one of the many voices bombarding me. He repeated his question. I kept praying, "Please God. I don't want to die. I want to get married and have kids. There is so much I haven't done yet."

"Remember to tell me when you feel something," the same doctor interrupted again.

"I don't," I mumbled, hoping he would understand that I meant I felt nothing. The doctor was quiet for a moment, then he asked me to raise my right leg. "Very good." Now raise your left leg. I did what he asked, desperately wishing he would leave me alone.

"No, Miss Coleman. Your left leg."

"I am raising my left leg."

"No, Miss Coleman. That's your right leg again." Irritated, I started to tune him out. I couldn't understand why he kept repeating commands when I was sure I was doing what he was asking. I went back to praying, deliberately ignoring the doctor. Finally, he told my parents they were taking me for an MRI, which I now know is a scan that looks at your brain.

I lay on the gurney listening to the monitor beeping. I was certain I was going to die. In the middle of this, my father kept saying, "Go to sleep Mary. Think of waterfalls and go to sleep." Lying there, I fought sleep as long as I could. My mind drifted between prayer and trying to block out TLC's song "Don't Go Chasing Waterfalls," which played in my brain as if the record was implanted there.

Early the next morning, I was awakened by a neurologist giving me the same commands from the night before. "You had a stroke," she said at the conclusion of her exam. Then she explained that damage from the stroke had completely paralyzed my left arm.

"When will I get better?" I asked, wishing my mother was with me. She was always good at getting all of the treatment instructions.

The doctor looked at me and said, "You may not ever get better."

I don't remember what else was said after that. What did she mean, I might not get better? I was mad at everything. I hated that I couldn't eat regular food. Everything I ordered from the hospital's menu came to me ground up like baby food because they believed my swallowing problem made me a choke risk. I thought they were wrong, even though I insisted the nurses crush my pills because they were too hard to swallow whole. Somehow, I didn't connect crushed pills to not being able to eat baked chicken from the hospital's menu, or see how my unstable balance made me a fall risk. I resented every rule that threatened my independence, so when two rehabilitation therapists came and told me they were admitting me to inpatient rehab the next morning, I had had enough of being told what to do, and rehab sounded like more of that, except ten times worse. I yelled and told them I wasn't going. When it became clear I wasn't going to sign the admission papers, they left saying, "Sleep on it. We'll talk some more tomorrow." I watched them leave.

Then I yelled at the closed door. "I'm not going. Tomorrow I'm 39. You can't make me!"

Shortly after breakfast, the entourage returned. "How are you doing, Mary?" one of the therapists asked in what I perceived as a sickly-sweet tone.

"Just fine." I wanted to match her tone, but all that came out was a monotone sound I barely recognized as my own.

Something was wrong with my voice. "I sound like a robot" ran through my mind as they described the wonders of rehab without convincing me to sign. As they turned to leave, I asked for my phone.

"It's right next to you," someone said.

"I don't see it." The therapist placed the phone in my hands and it was as if it had miraculously appeared. The stroke had left me with "left neglect," which meant I couldn't see anything on my left side. My brain only registered it once it was in my hand.

I'm not sure how long they stood outside my door whispering. I was preoccupied by the fact that I couldn't find my phone again. Later that evening my dad came to visit me.

"They say you won't go to rehab. Your mother and I think you should go."

"Why?" I asked.

"You need to go, so you can get better."

"They say I won't get better."

My dad sucked his teeth. "You can't listen to that. You will get better, but you have to go to rehab. Your mother can't come, so she sent me."

My mother's immune system was too low from her chemo treatments for stage IV lung cancer to enter the hospital. When my dad finally left, I was aware of two things: I was even more pissed off, and tomorrow I was going to rehab.

Rehab was even more like being in a bootcamp than I had suspected. I was awakened at 7 a.m. by the delivery of a breakfast tray. Then I was immediately thrown into the day's therapies.

First, came physical therapy (PT) where I spent what felt like endless hours relearning to walk without falling. Next came occupational therapy (OT). There I spent a lot of time learning to dress myself with one arm since my left one was completely paralyzed. In the beginning I thought this would be easy; how many times had I put on clothes or performed an act one-handed, but it's different when you can only rely on one hand. Finally, I went to speech therapy (ST) where I worked on varying my vocal range, so I wouldn't sound like a robot, and practiced exercises to strengthen my tongue and face muscles, so I could eat without choking. By the end of the first week of failing even the simplest cognitive and physical tests, I was exhausted and depressed. Every attempt led to failure after failure. That doctor was right. There is no way I can do this, I thought.

My OT could see my frustration when I walked into my session at the beginning of the second week. After a few exercises, she told me to focus and tell my brain to raise my left arm. "It won't," I said weakly, more defeated than angry. "You won't know until you try. Focus and ask your brain to do it." I sat there focused, praying my arm would move. Five minutes passed. Nothing. I threw my right arm up in defeat.

"Breathe. Now try again," the OT said calmly. I did and after what seemed like forever, my left arm raised as slowly as a security arm at a parking lot exit. It only raised a few inches, but it moved. I watched it slowly lower again. Then I smiled, silently thanking God and thinking, maybe, just maybe, things will get better.

My attitude changed drastically after that. I committed to work as hard as I could. My plan was to work 110% in rehab, go back to teaching, and in a year this whole nightmare would be over. Life would be normal again.

Except for the hard work, nothing went as I had planned. First, I was discharged from rehab and sent home to continue outpatient therapy after only two weeks. Then my ST questioned if I was really ready to return to work after she had me do a teaching demo. I had difficulty explaining the concepts and got frustrated with her interrupting me to ask nitpicky questions. When she pointed out she was just pretending to be a student, I snapped, "That's not fair. I'm skipping steps because I know you already know this."

Going home brought more stress. I had to be careful not to fall on the stairs or when taking a shower. I was also worried about my mother, who wasn't doing well after her last chemo treatment. She was worried about me, and I was worried about her practically every moment of that Thanksgiving weekend, which will forever be the worst one ever. My mother was too sick to cook, and I was too injured to help her. On November 28, I went into her room to check on her. She had barely eaten in two days.

"Mom, you need to eat something," I said gently.

"I will tomorrow," she replied softly, then added, "I'm more worried about you."

"Don't worry about me," I rushed to reassure her.

"I'll be fine, I promise I will, but you have to eat to get stronger." My mother's smile was too weak to reach her eyes.

Early that morning, my dad called and asked me to get my mother on the phone. I went into her room and called her, then shook her, but she didn't answer.

The rest of that morning turned out to be the worst of my life. My mother had died in her sleep. I went back to the phone in my room—who knows why I didn't just pick up the one next to her bed to tell my dad I couldn't wake her up. "I knew it," he cursed. "I'm on my way." For months after, I would wonder but never ask why he told me to wake her if he knew she had already passed. Why did I have to find her? At that moment, I went into autopilot, dialed 911, then watched the paramedics go into her room while gently pushing me out.

People often speak of traumas that rob them of breath and words, but words were all I had. Words and the air that gave them sound kept me upright while I waited and spoke to the crack in the door. In time, a paramedic came and told me, "I'm afraid your mother expired in the middle of the night." I went numb while I talked to the people from hospice and watched the funeral home carry my mother's body out as carefully as I'd been carried out to the ambulance five weeks prior. My mother was gone, and I didn't know how I could possibly keep my promise that I'd be fine. What I had meant was, I'll be fine as long as you're here with me. You're the one person I can count on to stand and battle for me when I can't.

Some say I'm strong, but I know my own strength was not enough to survive a massive stroke and my mother's death from stage IV lung cancer just over 30 days later. In a mere five weeks, my world had shattered, and it would take the grace of God, blessing me with the love and support of family and friends, to carry me through until I found the will—let alone the strength—to start putting the pieces back together again.

Elizabeth Arellano was born in Tucson, Arizona and raised in the remote town of Naco, Sonora. She is the youngest in her family and a first-generation college student. Elizabeth is currently attending community college and is set to transfer with honors in sociology. She is an inspiration to young student mothers and an advocate for higher education.

Elizabeth Arellano

Every Year Around Christmas

*To my family, friends, and Puente familia, who believed in me
before I ever did. For my brother Eduardo, who looks upon me.*

When a child is born, family and friends surround the parents with
words of encouragement, but when a child doesn't outlive his parents,
an overwhelming sense of injustice settles in the hearts and minds of the
family. A realization occurs, magnifying the loss of potential and unful-
filled dreams. Guilt builds and consumes the parents as a cancer. They
feel responsible for their child's death, no matter how irrational it may
seem because they have lost a vital part of their identity. It takes effort
to begin to live again, but with time the pain lessens, leaving only loving
memories.

Every year around Christmas my mother places a candle under the
portrait of the Virgen Maria and shares with us how she lost my older
brother, Eduardo. Placed at the corner of the living room mirror, there
is a picture of Eduardo jumping on the bed with his underwear over his
head, but that was a long time ago. When I was born, my parents became
very strict; they enforced curfews and they were afraid of everything,
afraid of us swimming, running, or jumping off of things like many children do.

Before I was born, my parents gave birth to two boys: Alejandro and
Eduardo. Alejandro was born with psychomotor impairment. His birth
defect was no surprise to my parents since an ultrasound had shown
abnormalities in my mother's womb. The doctors asked my parents
if they would like to terminate the pregnancy, but my mother, having

grown up with a brother who was disabled, felt no reason to do such a thing. But still my parents wanted to have a healthy baby boy, a boy who would conceive, pass down my father's name and be the inheritor of my father's wisdom. In order for my mother to conceive another child, she had to undergo therapy and take many vitamins. Their efforts came to fruition, and a healthy baby boy named Eduardo was born on September 24, 1988.

Eduardo era un travieso. At the time, they were living in Guadalajara, Jalisco and my mother recalls the day when Eduardo, Alejandro, and Rocío were playing outside while she was inside cooking. "I looked through the window and I saw your brothers playing inside the car. Eduardo, por supuesto, era el chofer. He moved the lever of the brake and the car started to move." My father sprinted down the steep hill chasing the car, jumping through the window and somehow managed to stop it. Luckily no one was hurt. Eduardo was not only travieso pero muy inquieto. He could not sit still for a single moment, unlike Alejandro who obeyed and mostly sat still quietly when told to do so.

The day tragedy struck our family was on December 19th, 1990. My father agreed to go to the store, and he took Alejandro and Eduardo with him to the liquor store located a short distance from the house. They entered the store and my father bought them some cookies and told them to sit still on the sidewalk while he went in and bought other groceries for the home. Alejandro sat still and obeyed while Eduardo got up and played around. He went into some bushes where an underground water well was located, covered only with cartón y lámina. My father exited the store and saw Alejandro sitting alone. He went home thinking Eduardo was there. Mad, my father asked for my brother, but my mother had no idea where he was. They looked for him all over the neighborhood, and my mother thought he might have been kidnapped. A search party was formed, consisting of family and neighbors. It was getting dark and they had not found him. A neighbor went towards the bushes where my brother had been playing. He asked the owner of the store if the tank was filled with water, but he answered, "No, está un poco vacía." He asked for a flashlight and looked into a small opening in the laminate. It was then that they saw my brother floating in the water, unconscious. My dad rushed and tried to enter, but he was too big for the small gap. A young thin gentleman entered the tank and grabbed my brother. My brother still held the cookies my dad had bought him in his left hand. The tank was mostly empty as the owner previously mentioned, but there was enough water to cover a two-year-old standing all the way to the nose. My mother watched her son's unconscious body lying on the floor as my father gave him CPR. The ambulance arrived, and my mother pleaded to know if he was going to be okay. My dad reassured her that everything was going to be fine, but in her heart she knew he was gone.

The ambulance left with Eduardo and my father onboard. They arrived at the hospital, and my brother's body was going to be thrown on the floor in a room full of people who had passed away in the hospital, but my father did not let them. He held Eduardo's cold body close to him and hugged him as if were alive. Placing him on a surgical table and taking his clothes off gently, he stayed with his body until it was time to bring him home.

Eduardo was brought home in a brown, wooden coffin by my father and placed in the living room. My mother walked in and saw his lifeless body. She looked up to the ceiling and said, "Si eres diós lo levantarás con una sola palabra," but nothing happened. During my brother's funeral, my father placed his lips on his forehead, hugging him and pleading for forgiveness, believing it was his fault rather than a tragic accident. My mother, on the other hand, could not do the same. She stood across the room away from the coffin because she wanted to leave with the image of her son playing around the house as he had that morning. Alejandro could not comprehend what had happened. During the service Rocío went towards my mother and told her, "Mami, Eduardo is not dead; he is just sleeping." In that moment my mother collapsed to the floor crying inconsolably.

After the burial my mother fell into a deep depression. She spent many days lying in bed, and my father worked long hours to avoid being home. Rocío took care of Alejandro the best way she could. Christmas passed and the presents stayed unopened. Decorations remained hanging around the house for the following months until the summer of 1991 when Rocio and Alejandro were finally able to open their presents. My mother opened Eduardo's present; it was an action figure on a motorcycle. This toy was chosen by Eduardo in a clothing store months before his passing. To this day it still remains on a shelf, untouched.

Within one year after Eduardo died, my mother gave birth to Sandra on November 2, 1991. My mother loved her, but my father could not be around her for the first few days after she was born. It seemed like my brother had been reincarnated, as Sandra was the exact same image of Eduardo, but with time, my father grew to love her. Now Sandra is married and carries her first child, who will be named Eduardo.

Chris is a dedicated counselor who serves underrepresented youth and communities in San Diego County. He is an appreciative, loving husband and a proud father of two beautiful girls.

Chris

Kaiya

This piece is dedicated to the parents and kids struggling on Autism Island.

Kai, Hawaiian for ocean. Ya, Korean suffix used for endearment.

Together the sea of love that surrounds us all, Kaiya.

Time to wake up: It's a school day today. Kaiya's eyes are heavy because of her insomnia and playing Barbies with Papa at three in the morning. Need to get up, though, because Kaiya needs to earn her button, and ten buttons equal a toy on Friday. She gets up, and it's time to get dressed. Clothes need to be all pink, head to toe, and shirt needs to be a tank top. That's right. No sleeves, no matter what the weather. We go downstairs, and the smell of Mommy's fried rice fills the room. Time for braids, two braids to be exact. Has to be two braids. She's looking cute with her self-cut bangs, and now it's time for school, but Mommy and Kaiya are late as usual. Late arrival at school, and Kaiya receives her usual red card for being tardy, but Mommy got her there, and that's a struggle in itself.

◆ ◆ ◆

The school day consists of learning letters, numbers, and songs with her friend Ema, the only other girl in her class. After school, Mommy picks her up, and she is full of joy. Now they are off to speech therapy with Mrs. Napour, her speech therapist since the beginning. Mrs. Napour loves her some Kaiya. They play and work on using words to build useful sentences. After speech therapy, they come home to meet with Sammy, her applied behavior analysis (ABA) therapist, who has also been with Kaiya for the last three years. Sammy loves her some Kaiya, too. They play with the neighborhood friends and work on socially acceptable behaviors and understanding social cues. After ABA, Papa comes home from work, and it's time to play. Papa loves him some Kaiya, also. Tag, zombies, dancing, Barbies, bubbles, whatever she feels like doing, usually all of it. Mommy makes dinner, and it needs to be chicken and rice. Nothing else.

After dinner, it's time for homework. Writing letters and numbers with a special-grip pencil that has helped a lot, but the letters "d" and "b" can be tricky. Homework is done and one more button for the toy. We make it through homework without a meltdown, and now it's time to get ready for bed, but showers can be tricky, too. Another button to get through. PJ time! PJs have been the same bees-and-queens shirt for the last three years. Yes, we have to find the same shirt and buy it in bigger sizes as she grows. It's her favorite shirt, and Kaiya can't sleep without it. Brush the teeth, read a book, and get as much sleep as possible to do it all again tomorrow.

◆ ◆ ◆

January 30th, 2012, my wife Jennifer's water broke. This was our second child, so we were prepared. Everything was going smoothly, when unexpectedly our baby's heart stopped beating. The nurses rushed Jennifer into the delivery room, and I was forced to wait outside. The doctors were performing an emergency cesarean. I paced back and forth with no communication from anyone. My wife's and daughter's lives were in their hands. All kinds of things ran through my head as I held myself back from jumping in that room. Twenty minutes later a nurse comes out and says, "Mr. Toomey, you can see your wife." I run to Jennifer as the doctors continue to stitch her up, and I hold her hand as she cries, "Is my baby okay?" I look over the sheet blocking the view to our baby, and doctors and nurses continue to surround our baby. "No, No." This can't be happening. We're losing our baby. Then comes the cry of life that turns our tears of fright into tears of joy. She made it! Kaiya Akimi is here.

The roller coaster of emotions took place in a matter of 20 minutes and left us drained. We remained in the hospital the next few days to recover, and the doctor said Kaiya was fine. Kaiya was a difficult baby, and we thought maybe we had just had it easy with her older sister, Nicole. Kaiya liked to watch basketball with me for hours, and I thought she would be the next WNBA superstar, but something strange was going on. She never made any attempt to connect with us or make sounds like typical babies. She didn't look at us, attempt to play with us or engage us in any type of exchange. Her first birthday came, and Kaiya still had no words or attempts to connect. We thought she might be a bit delayed and, of course, all our family and friends would say the same. "Don't worry about it, she's fine." We would go to the park, and rather than play at the playground with the other kids, she would wander off and climb the fence or make snow angels in the dirt. At home, she would take objects and put them into long straight lines across the floor. Peculiar, but we didn't think about it too often. Looking back, maybe we were in denial. Kaiya's second birthday came, and she still had no words or attempts to connect. We started to question, "Is there something wrong with Kaiya?" All our friends and family continued to say the same thing, "She's fine," but what did they know? This was our baby.

We made an appointment with the doctor, and the doctor watched Kaiya as she ignored him and attempted to climb up everything in the examination room, including the doctor. Kaiya fixated on the doctor's stethoscope and would not stop. It was like Kaiya didn't even take into consideration that she was climbing on a person. The doctor says to us that she would like to schedule some more appointments and tests, "just to be safe." Just to be safe from what? The doctor says, "Kaiya may have autism," and I think, "No way!" I had worked with autistic kids 15 years prior, and I am in complete denial that Kaiya could end up like Joshua, an autistic client I had worked with. Joshua punched, scratched, bit, engaged in repetitive fixations, and couldn't speak a word at age 15. Joshua and I made progress, but "progress" meant learning how to sit in class without throwing chairs and running out. He could hardly function in everyday life. Is this what the doctor is saying Kaiya is going to be like? We go home, and I can't stop looking at her as my mind starts to race like it has never raced before. I get no sleep and go to work as if everything is okay, but it's not.

Later that week we meet with the doctor, and she goes over the process. We receive a ten-page questionnaire and schedule an observation for Kaiya. The observation consists of five different specialized doctors watching Kaiya play with an assistant and then some one-on-one time with her. The questionnaire was ridiculous in our opinion. For the most part, all we kept saying as we filled it out was, "This applies to all kids." Again, maybe we were deep in denial. Some of the questions did hit us though and had us questioning whether Kaiya had autism. We couldn't answer any of the questions when it came to anything verbal. I could see the tears in Jennifer's eyes, but it still had not hit me.

Jennifer takes Kaiya to the observation and turns in the questionnaire. I ask how the observation went, and Jennifer tells me that they didn't say anything. Again, we are in the dark. We wait weeks as the doctors need to deliberate and write up their final report. Our house was always full of cheer and life, but those weeks we sat in silence.

The time comes to meet the doctor to go over the report. We leave Kaiya with her sister and make our way to the doctor's office. The doctor explains the process of how the decision is made, but she sees that we don't care to hear it at this point. She pauses and simply states that Kaiya has autism. Jennifer starts to cry, and the doctor hands her a box of tissue that she has ready by her side. I freeze, drop my head, and tears start uncontrollably running down my face. My emotions take over and I lose control of myself, as I can't stop the tears. My heart hurts like I never felt before. The doctor wipes her own tears and starts to explain what we can do and the support services available, but we are not in the place to listen to any of it. She hands us the report and some phone numbers, and we head home. The tears keep coming as we drive home; our baby girl is sick, and we can't do anything about it.

As a man, I want to fix it and make Kaiya better. I fixed my fucked-up life, and as a counselor I helped youths put their lives together, but autism? I can't fix that, and thoughts of Joshua start to run through my head, and I can't see past that. That's when things start to turn for the worse, as my mind starts to run with all kinds of negative thoughts. I can't sleep, I'm not eating right, and I begin to disconnect. Unable to cope, old demons begin to surface, and I start to drink heavily to numb the pain. Jennifer, on the other hand, is a champion. She grieves for a couple weeks and begins her journey as supermom while I begin my journey into a deep hole. Kaiya's sister, Nicole, takes all of it in stride and begins her research to answer the question she kept asking, "What is autism?"

Jennifer makes appointments with the San Diego Regional Center to get ABA therapy, speech therapy, as well as to enroll Kaiya into preschool for autistic kids. She takes Kaiya to all of her appointments. I, on the other hand, find any excuse to go get a drink, and when I'm home I spend most of my time smoking cigarettes to calm myself down. My mind says, "Fuck ABA therapy. That shit doesn't help." I used to do therapy with clients, and it had very little effect. Speech therapy doesn't sound prom-ising, as they play games at therapy just like we do at home. My mind is in a state of trauma, and everything is negative. My thoughts are if we can't help her then no one can, and if I can't help my own daughter, then I fail as a parent. Just like that, I put myself into a vicious cycle in which I would always come out losing. Nicole and Jennifer try to engage and comfort me, but neither of them know what to do. Jennifer has her hands full with Kaiya, and Nicole is busy being a senior in high school.

I feel myself disconnecting and watch Jennifer take it upon herself to do it all. She wouldn't ask me to help, but I could see her disappointment in me. I decide to take on something I do know, and that's school systems. I put in formal writing to request an IEP (individualized education plan) evaluation and submit Kaiya's diagnosis report that states she has autism. With the request in writing, the school is required to meet with us. We have the meeting, and in the room are the speech pathologist, special education coordinator, teacher, administrator, and school psychologist. Six different educators against me, as they question the need for Kaiya to be accepted for special education services. Schools do this because a student who qualifies for services costs the district money and time, but the law requires it. I know this because I am on the other side of the table as a school employee. After the meeting, I call everyone I know that is connected to special education services in the district, just to make sure. I'm beginning to feel like a champion except that every time I speak about Kaiya the tears start. I can't seem to move forward. The medical diagnosis is enough, and I know this, but I allow the school to go through their complicated process, and it's a waiting game again. A few weeks later I get the call stating Kaiya qualifies, and they would like me to come in to sign off on the IEP. The IEP consists of goals like, "Kaiya will respond seven out of ten times when called by her name," and "Kaiya will be able to say 'yes' or 'no' five out of ten times when asked a question." We come up with these goals together as a team. The IEP-for-free preschool at the public school also includes speech therapy provided by the school, free door-to-door bus transportation, a specialized autism class with fewer students, more teacher aids, and an extended school year. I did it, but I am still in pain.

I let my principal and director know what's going on, but they don't seem to understand what I am going through. My principal has a child with Asperger's, a type of autism, and the director is a former school psychologist who's married to a school psychologist who specializes in early childhood intervention. Neither of them helps, but help in my head at the time is a cure. Give me the cure. Nobody has the cure, so I drink. I still can't sleep well, and I am trying to function on two to four hours of sleep. I'm not much help even when I try to be. When Kaiya is scratching us, biting us, screaming, biting the wall, chewing on the dining table, all I can do is notice all the crazy shit going on, and I feel even more hopeless as a father.

I know my drinking is getting out of hand when I hang out with people I don't even like or people I don't know. I am hurt and disconnected, but I am still aware of my present state. The hopeless feeling is there, but I know I can do something. Jennifer says, you're killing yourself and your daughter needs you, but I'm not listening. I'm coming home at four, five, and six in the morning on a weekday, and it serves me right that Jennifer threatens to leave my ass. She doesn't, and instead says a prayer every night for me that I get better and go back to the fun-loving man that she married—the one who tells stories and entertains the family, the one that motivates and inspires, the one that stays connected and gives all the love he has.

We all know God works in mysterious ways, and I receive a call from a friend with a job opportunity. I immediately jump on it. I know getting a second job would allow Jennifer to stay home full time and take care of Kaiya. Having Jennifer at home taking care of Kaiya would put my mind at ease. I also know that it would eliminate the number of times I go out to drink. I get the job and the drinking starts to fade, but the pain is still there. The second job keeps me at work from 7 a.m. to 8 p.m., but I have switched vices to do the same thing: avoid. From alcoholic to workaholic, but I'm not drinking. I have started to heal with the help of the people I trust.

With so much on my mind, even when I am home I am still disconnected. Physically I'm there, but not the kind of father and husband that I am capable of being. Sober, I start to see how I need to make an effort to reconnect or I will lose them both. I start my fight to accept Kaiya's autism and work with her. Being a parent of an autistic child is difficult. For us, Kaiya's disconnection and inability to verbalize left us in the dark. When she's sick, it's a guessing game and frequent visits to the hospital. When she tantrums, it's like playing charades with someone who isn't really playing. Everything you teach your kids or communicate to your kids does not apply because she has no language. The mental breakdowns are at a different level and I don't judge people for keeping their autistic kids at home, but we refuse and together we take Kaiya out as much as possible to get her to connect. To bring the Kaiya that is in there out, we can't let anything stop us. We live on Autism Island, and we will build as many bridges as we need to. She may not speak, but she is thinking. She may not make eye contact, but she sees you. She may not understand, but she feels you.

The difficulty of being a parent of a child with autism is something that is hard to comprehend for many. The difficulties will always be there as a parent, but it is not as difficult as having autism. I watch Kaiya fight every day to learn, connect, and play. She lives life in her own special way, and I am learning to appreciate it all. Kaiya tantrums because she cares and she is fighting to communicate. Today she says "hi" to everyone in the neighborhood. When I'm on the phone, she always wants to say "hi" to anyone I'm on the phone with. Supermom Jennifer attracted the neighborhood kids with popsicles, and now Kaiya has friends she plays with daily. Her speech is improving by copying what others say and can apply it as she memorizes it. Her speech therapy is working. She is learning the interaction with others because her ABA therapy is working. Kaiya does swimming, gymnastics, dance, karate, and is currently in kindergarten. She receives fives in school and does homework at night. Her sister Nicole has been accepted to Cal State San Marcos's speech pathology program, works two jobs, and comes home to visit as much as she can. One of her jobs is working with children with autism, and she plans to become a speech pathologist working with kids with autism in the future. I am in a better place of acceptance and living up to what I can be. Being a good father and husband takes a lot of effort, especially when you didn't have one yourself. I will continue to fight like Kaiya to be the best I can be. We all advocate for Kaiya because we want her to advocate for herself. As a family, we are blessed to witness a miracle every day as Kaiya grows, and as Kaiya grows, she helps us all grow.

During the time of the following events, **Leticia** was between 12 and 17 years old. She is 18 years old now, attending San Diego City College, and she is very happy to be there because she didn't know she would make it this far. She still writes, though not as much, and has picked up drawing again. She hopes to make it really far in life and to continue healing.

Leticia Alatorre Ramirez

Bright Desolation

*I would like to dedicate my story to everyone who feels alone,
misread, and misunderstood, and to everyone who has been through
similar experiences and persevered. It is also for our fallen brothers
and sisters who couldn't make it.*

Middle school was going well until we had to suffer through some
tragedies, and I faced some hard issues as well. Sixth grade, my cousin
Adrian drowned in his house pool; seventh grade, my cousin Jasmine
died in a car crash; and right at the beginning of eighth grade, my
grandpa died of lung cancer. Through the years I was bullied, called
names I would rather not repeat, and I was pushed around. Being a shy
and scared child, I never knew how to stand up for myself, so I took the
pain. I started to close myself off, and I wouldn't let any friends get close
to me. I wouldn't let them touch me or see inside my heart. By freshman
year everything was so dark and desolate. The voices that insulted me
would echo in the back of my mind. They seemed to surround me and
follow me everywhere I went. I had blood-rush nightmares and sinister
ideas that never left but only got worse.

My relationship with my mother was ruined because, in hopes of
saving my skin, I had started lying and not letting her see what was going
on with me. But one day I decided to confide in her.

"Everything feels really fake, and I just want to put something sharp
on my skin and just start scratching it until I start bleeding." I'm guessing
she wasn't thinking much of it.

"Go ahead," she said.

What happened next, she wasn't ready for.

I started wearing long sleeve shirts and sweaters, but it wasn't until I was caught changing that my mother saw the scars. Angry like a bull with smoke coming out of her nose and ears, she stared at me like a red target. She stomped her feet and seemingly charged forward. Grabbing my wrist with an iron grip, she yanked my arm so hard it almost popped out of my shoulder socket. Her hot breath burned my face, and her voice echoed in my brain. "What are you doing? Why are there scars on your wrist?"

I couldn't seem to form any words, and before I knew it, I wasn't looking at her face anymore. No, I was staring at the side of my bed. I could feel my cheek stinging, and my eyesight blurred. She left words ringing in the background,

"For every fresh cut, I will hit you!" Everything came crashing down after that day.

You're probably wondering why I ever decided to pick up a razor and cut. I'll tell you why. It gave me a sense of being and knowing that I was alive. It was a way for me to be relieved from everything I kept inside,,,,,,, and it brought me comfort. It was a euphoric feeling, and it made me happy. If you asked me how, I wouldn't know how to describe it.

At one point, realizing that I wouldn't have the pleasure of having my mom find me dead, I called 911. I was thinking of my grandma and my cousins. How would my grandma feel if she knew her grandchild ended her own life? How would my cousins that look up to me react if they were told the real reason for my passing? It didn't seem fair.

My mother would inflict pain on me. I started thinking she didn't love me and that she wished I never existed, so I continued cutting and watching the blood run down my wrist. That seemed to give me comfort, but it was a vicious cycle that lasted a long while.

By my junior year in high school I was fed up with everything and everyone. I was so closed off that people were scared to talk or even look at me. People got so used to me being antisocial that I practically became invisible. Only some, my close friends, were able to see me. One day I decided I had had enough of everything and everyone. I was convinced this life was fake and that if I ended it all I would be able to wake up from the coma I had been in. I could then live the life that had been taken away.

Once I got home I took the razor. I gave my skin some love, and I rummaged through everything trying to find the sleeping pills. When I couldn't find them, I added some more cuts to my wrist. Knowing that I wouldn't have the pleasure of having my mother find me strung out on the floor overdosed on sleeping pills with bloody wrists, I called 911 again. I was taken to the emergency room. It took my mother a while to find me at the hospital, and even though she was angry, she was just as worried for my life.

After a quick intervention, a 5150 hold was suggested, and I was delivered to Mesa Vista Hospital. A 5150 hold means that a clinician or an officer is able to involuntarily confine a person suspected to have a mental disorder to a psychiatric institution if determined to be a danger to themselves or others. I made that place my home, and I was glad to be there. I could get away from all my issues and the outside world. I stayed there for a week before going home, but I seemed to do worse when I was out.

My mother tried taking me to church because she thought Jesus could save me. I felt sick to my stomach, and couldn't help but think, "How can you be so stupid? Jesus can't save me or fix me." I sat through the sermon without paying attention and rushed out at the end like a blazing fire. Instead of following me, my mom stayed behind and said "Hi" to the whole damned church.

I subconsciously made the decision to get better on my own. I began to crack a couple smiles here and there and tried talking to new people. Although I still had my flaws talking to others and keeping my anxiety low, I was able to make improvements and make some new friends. I surrounded myself with good caring and positive friends. I learned to lean on someone when I needed help, but even though I've learned all this, I still keep my emotions caged, and I don't let anyone touch my feelings.

I can't exactly say I'm fully healed and completely happy, but I think I would be truly happy if I had a sense of closure from my father—to ask him why it is that he left me, why he never wanted to try being a part of my life, and why he never wanted to see me. I would also have loved the experience of having siblings, but I know that is not possible because my father left and my mother had to go through some hard times to get me to where I am today. I know at the end of the day people are asking themselves what advice I would give others or what I would tell anyone else that is going through similar experiences. I would like to let them know that I know how it feels. I know what it's like to be kicked when you're down and how it feels when no one around you seems to care or understand.

Society thinks of us as weak people and that we are just too stuck in our minds, but no one seems to understand the issues we go through because everyone else is living a dandy life. It may seem like the end of the world, or that everyone is out to get you to stitch a smile on your face, but there are some of us who understand. Keeping a journal at my side has helped me a lot; I've written a lot of poems and short stories pertaining to my emotions of a particular event. It may be hard for your parents to understand, but if you give them a sense of what's going on, in time they will be aware of what's happening. In the meantime, surround yourself with people you love—people who are positive and those who care about you and your well-being. Go out on adventures with friends and live life to the fullest.

Lina Kern is the mother of two boys, who grew up in the Oak Park community of San Diego. Having been heavily impacted by community violence and drug use, Lina decided to pursue studies in psychology so she could help heal the neighborhood she grew up in. She currently works with other young single mothers.

Lina Kern
Not My Burden to Carry

*I dedicate this story to Juan, my mentor, for his strength to hold
my hand during this process; to my kiddos, who taught me the true
definition of unconditional love; and lastly to my partner, who has
been my rock because without him I would not have been able to tell
my story.*

Like most young girls I used to dream of the day Prince Charming would
come sweep me off my feet. I never imagined what he would look like,
but I always fantasized about the way he would make me feel. I've always
had a tough time opening up to others, so I knew that Prince Charming
would be the one I could talk to about anything. I imagined he would be
the stranger I would recognize, the one who knew how to make me smile
and put my soul at ease.

I still remember the way he brought butterflies to my stomach. I had
never known a comfort so sweet as I would gently rest my head on his
shoulder. I thought to myself, "This is it. This is what love must feel like."
There was only one time I had felt this kind of comfort before, and that
was in my previous relationship. I knew this time was different.

My previous relationship quickly diminished when I disclosed that
I was not ready for his sexual advances. Although my ex-boyfriend had
initially respected where I was at, it quickly became a focal point in our
relationship. Ultimately, I felt heartbroken when I was given an ultima-
tum: either we would become intimate with one another, or we needed
to part ways. Needless to say, we parted ways.

This relationship was different to me. This relationship was the one I had been dreaming about. I also knew if I was open and honest about my boundaries that I would be "doing things the right way." I was very direct about what I was comfortable with, what was off limits and what I needed to make this experience feel safe and secure. After several intimate conversations we both seemed to be on the same page.

I was thankful to have found someone so understanding. I was also looking forward to all the cute things that were about to enter my life. I could not wait to wake up next to the man I loved. I was finally going to get the chance to explore the parts of myself that were meant to be shared with my other half. I was most excited to be able to fall asleep in his arms and be woken up by his angel kisses and warm touch.

No one prepared me for what I was about to experience. There were no angel kisses. The shoulder that once felt so safe had now turned cold. The warmth of his tender touches had soon disappeared, and what was left was confusion. As a person who doesn't open up easily, I spent a lot of time in my head analyzing my own thoughts and emotions.

I would replay everything in my head over and over again. I would replay the night that the condom broke because I knew he had put it on. I had made it very clear that was one of my boundaries that I was not willing to negotiate. It wasn't until years later I found out that he had taken it off intentionally. I would replay the nights he ignored my needs as he turned his back to me. I began questioning why he would pressure me, persistently, to try new things I voiced I was not comfortable with.

I remember telling one of my closest friends how I felt bad because I would reject the idea of being woken up to sex. Her response was "GIRL! I love that shit." That reaction only solidified the idea that I needed to get out of my own head and learn to be a better partner. Until one night I woke up to him on top of me and all I could do was cry. Like a prisoner in my own mind, I couldn't formulate the words to express how truly violated I felt, over and over again.

Our relationship ended shortly after, not because of how I felt but because he ended up moving and I wasn't willing to follow. I never consciously gave my experience much thought. Subconsciously, I knew it was impacting me, but I would tell myself it was merely an experience, nothing more, nothing less. It was a time in my life where I was figuring out who I was, what I liked and what I didn't like. He was my boyfriend, he loved me, and naturally we would share experiences with one another as we explored our own wants and needs. I still felt that I hadn't been the best girlfriend due to how I was reacting to him.

It wasn't until years later when I entered my Master's in Counseling program that everything would resurface. We were assigned a writing project that would have us explore many different aspects of ourselves, including intimacy and sexuality. I was brutally honest and wrote about the hurt, betrayal, guilt, shame, and violation I was still carrying with me from those experiences when I was younger. This writing exercise was more than ten pages, front and back, and of all the feedback I had received there was only one comment I remember: "That's sexual abuse."

All the confusion I had once felt came flooding back accompanied by endless questions. I wrestled with the idea of sexual abuse for more than six months before ever speaking on it. As I stumbled over the words to describe what I was going through, I found that I was still defending him: he was innocent, he didn't mean it, he didn't know…he was my boyfriend.

I struggle with the term sexual abuse because I do not consider myself a victim nor a survivor of sexual abuse. There is, however, a great deal of freedom that has come from those two words. I now have the language and words to describe my experience and recognize it for what it truly was. Understanding rape and sexual abuse as well as the emotions that accompanied my experience has allowed me to regain my power. It has allowed me to feel empowered.

I still wrestle with the facts and facing the truth, not because it didn't happen or because I am in denial, but because it still has some lingering effects. I realize it's time to take back my story and tell it. I know there are many other women who have a story that's hidden, buried beneath the guilt and shame of their experiences. This isn't my burden to carry anymore. There is no need for guilt or shame, just room for healing and connecting with others.

DJ Kuttin Kandi is a "People's Hip Hop DJ Scholar" who was born and raised in Queens, NY and is widely regarded as one of the most legendary and accomplished womxn DJs in the world. Kandi is a disabled Filipinx-Pin[a/x]y-American queer, writer, poet, theater performer, educator, hip-hop feminist, and community organizer. In 2018, DJ Kuttin Kandi was titled a Global Hip Hop and Cultural Ambassador by Next Level's Meridian International Center, the University of North Carolina at Chapel Hill, and the US Department of State's Bureau of Educational and Cultural Affairs. She currently serves as an alternate site manager for Next Level. She is a known pop-culture political essayist and has written for several anthologies and blogs, including as a guest contributing writer for *Colorlines*, *Racialicious*, and more. Kandi is also the co-editor of the book *Empire of Funk: Hip Hop & Representation in Filipino/a America* and is currently co-editing a new anthology on Pin[a/x]y activism, releasing in Spring 2021.

Heart Surrender

The Count, The Beat, and the Battle to Get There

I looked up at the ceiling as I heard him stomp around and rumble through the boxes that were stored in the hidden side doors of the attic. I looked back at the loudly playing television as I sat still in the living room contemplating if I should go up the stairs to ask him if he needed help.

I stared out into the kitchen and reminisced about the sounds of clatter and chopping that used to fill the room. I thought about how the home that was once filled with 26 Filipinx immigrants was now empty and how the scent of my Lola's fried tilapia was no longer present, as she and Lolo had moved into my Auntie Nancy's new apartment across the way. It was just two months ago when my father, a sick cancer patient, had had a fight with my grandfather, just after he returned home to New York City from his six-month proton beam treatment out in Loma Linda. The fist fight led to my grandparents having to move out of the house, as it was not safe for either of them, nor was it safe for my chemo-treated father to be dealing with any stressful situations.

"Candice, can you come upstairs?" my father called out to me. I sighed, got up from the couch, and climbed up the carpeted stairs to the attic.

"What are you looking for, Daddy?" I asked, almost afraid to look around my sister's turned-upside-down room from all the things my father pulled out from the side storage. "I'm looking for my old wooden mixer that I used to play with my stereo system." I had no idea what he was talking about, but I ducked down to squeeze myself through the storage doors.

"Nevermind," he said and rubbed his bald head. "I'm tired and I need water," he said, exhausted.

As I crept back out of the tiny storage space, I looked up at my father, who now wore a patch over his eye, as he had lost his eyesight due to the rare tumor that rested between the nerve of his eye and spinal cord. "Don't worry, Daddy, I'll find it for you."

◆ ◆ ◆

It would be the next year that I did my first DJ artist tour. Another year later, my mother lost her job of 22 years. Two years later, we lost our home.

What is home anyway, especially when I was busy running away from the supposed safe haven that my family thought they were providing me? It's not like I didn't have family tryin' to call me to come back. It's not like they ever stopped searching for me. They always brought me back home, even when my father once put a big ol' mattress at the side door entrance tryin' to prevent me from coming back into the house. Did they want me home or not?

I never understood the push and pull of microaggressions. Nor did I ever understand being a young ten-year-old child on the left of my sleeping Lola as my grandfather molested me under the covers. For years, I battled with never bringing hiya (shame) to the family. So I stayed stuck between the "don't air out the dirty laundry" code and the urge to find home and create new family.

Thus, I found family in music. It was almost as if my beating heart knew it had to lead me right to those silver platters. The heart knew it had to guide me right at home with those two turntables.

I remember coming home after school and walking into my bedroom with all of my things thrown onto the floor. All of my clothes had been tossed off the bed, books were off the shelves, and the mattress was off the rail of the bed. I ran down the stairs to find out who the heck thrashed up my room. Just when I was about to turn into the kitchen, that's when I got got hit across the arm and fell to the couch. Bam.

"Don't you ever take my jacket ever again!" my father yelled at me. I couldn't even look up at him because I was wincing from the pain and holding up my arm. Tears fell down as I crunched up into a ball to protect myself because I was afraid he was going to hit me again. I stared down at the long and large silver metal plumbing tool he held in his hand. Part of me was still in disbelief that he had hit me with such a big and heavy tool. The other part of me was in rage that he was beating me up over his leather jacket because I had taken it from his closet and worn it to school. He had hit me so many times over the years that I would often flinch whenever he came into the room. The patriarchy in me still excuses it and claims that I deserved such treatment each time I had failed him and mother. Discipline is what he'd always say, while my mother often laid in the cut, noddin' in agreement.

The truth is, it's when you've been beaten down like this that you lose all understanding of what home even means. "Dumb" and "stupid" were popular nicknames, and "I love you" was never a common phrase. Unless of course, you get caught smoking cigarettes, get yelled at for selling and smokin' weed, get kicked out of the house and then asked to come back. Tears in my father's eyes and everything, "You know that I love you...." I saw the hurt in his eyes, and I felt the hurt in his heart. I truly believed he was authentic with his weak apologies every time he kicked me out of the house while my Lola, my heroine, always tried to save me. In any case, I found myself always hurting, as he was hurting in dealing with whatever baggage he was carrying. But I was sixteen years old, and it was something I couldn't carry for him. At the time, I didn't quite know the rumblings of being gaslit, but I knew the fire was treacherous, and I couldn't deal with the ways I was made to be the one wrong or "crazy" all the time. Nor could I handle the way the cops were always called on me by my own family every time I perpetuated the same anger I learned from them. Disposability will throw a woman right into the pit that leaves her not only as the harmed but as the very oppressor she never wanted to become.

That same fire thrust me right into the arms of broken lovers who beat out every song I ever knew. I clung to drugged-up and drunken nights spent with those I didn't know and with ones who certainly didn't deserve me. I reached for the lovers who continued to make me question myself when I knew exactly where I belonged. I stayed in an eight-year relationship that had me believing that love was a war story filled with "cuts for luck." But, as always, I beat dropped Mystic's "Ghetto Birds" song and reminisced of a lover's tale.

Music is the grey area. It's the place where I find and lose myself amidst the rhythm and the blues. It's about the breath I take before I enter a plane. It's that coolness that I felt right at the hit of a white line, or it's that slow pull of a blunt that I need to have on the daily. It's the guilt that my ten-year-old self carries, who remembers trying to push her sister out the second-story window. It's the seconds that I laid desperately waiting for someone to believe me and save me from my #metoo moment. It's the moments that I grieve my cousin's death by suicide and the years that I spend trying to forgive myself for trying to do the same. It's the degree of the anger that my clenched fists won't let go of whenever I am deep in another lovers' quarrel. It's the duration of a chant and the long march to freedom with a thousand comrades I've never met. It's the moments that I continue to search for my reflection off the glimmer of an ocean wave.

It wasn't until I had to undergo open heart surgery that I may have caught a glimpse of who my father was. I was exposed to the judgment and ridicule of the doctors and the scrutiny of the bright lights beating down on me. His words hit me, "Do you know what it feels like for me when doctors look at me and judge me because they know the reason I'm sick is that I was a smoker but yet never say anything to me?" I shudder as I remember hearing him choking on his tears when he caught me smoking cigarettes.

Is this what it felt like for my father when he underwent countless medical treatments and experiments, as he had gone through cancer twice in his life? Did he have the same questions as I did? Did he cringe at the way they touched him and loathe the way they examined him in silence, all while knowing full well they were judging him? Did he imagine himself as a cow being huddled into claustrophobic laboratory corners? Was he held by anyone the way I wanted to be held? Did he carry the same self-guilt and self-blame as I did? Did he want to take moments back, wish for the chance to redo everything like I did? Did he hold regrets the same way I carried dreams deferred? Did he try to look into his doctor's eyes to find some kind of compassion, as I searched for a hint of kindness from mine?

Did he count the minutes and the seconds for every test result to come back? Did he look at the clock the way I did and learn the way it ticks when you wait for friends and other loved ones to come visit you? Was he sorry for all the things that led him to that path? Was he sorry for everything he never got to say to me? Did he battle the same way I summoned nightmares? Or did he surrender the heart like the way my arms were longing to reach for the almighty sky?

I would never know. I only knew what little my mother had shared.

"I'm sorry. I'm sorry for the things I was never able to do for you. I'm sorry that I never got to take you anywhere and buy you beautiful things. I'm sorry that I won't be there to see our children grow up or to walk them down the aisle. I'm sorry that I didn't give you the life I wanted to give you..." my father cried to my mother as he looked into her eyes from the hospital bed. She cried back, "Please don't be sorry. You gave me everything. You gave me everything."

A service worker who waited on tables at catering parties part-time, my father barely made enough to make a dent and get our family out of debt. In the face of no college degree, piling bills due to medical treatments, a thick Pilipino accent, and my mother's entire family to feed, my father worked hard and gave his all. Despite my father's shortcomings and inner battle, I always saw the many layers about him. It wasn't hard to see the good things about him, as there was tenderness and depth to the subtle ways he showed up for us. There was gentleness in how he adored us from afar though he never uttered a gentle word of love. It showed up in the ways he prepared large family meals for us and eagerly sought the approval of my Lola and Lolo on his cooking. It was with my father, not my mother, that I always had the deep conversations about life. Not only that, my father was the one who actually cut my mother's frequent verbal put-downs against my sister and me. He was the one who I'd often find myself trying to dig to the core of, just so I could understand that tough poor little city boy from Cavite in Manila, Philippines.

Like my father who loved music and collected records, I dug into record crates and searched for the rarity of sweet moments that I intensely yearned. I looked for the man that I had seen that one cold, snowy blizzarding morning who helped dig a family and their station wagon out of six feet of snow, even as he was weak from chemo treatments. I longed for the few and far in-between 45s that comforted me and reaffirmed everything I couldn't say. I closed my eyes, leaned back, and related to the sounds of Clarence Carter's "Patches" and ached the way Gladys Knight did when she sang out, "This child needs its father, come back home...." Through this heart-wrenching digging and soul-collecting search, I was able to turn every broken heart of mine by every lover that shattered me into my own lyrical song.

I don't want like I used to. I do, however, cut records. I cut them like poetry spinning off the wheels of my turntables. I play records like songs trying to reach their climactic reasoning and beat juggle them as they work their way to the break to find some kind of justice out of their rhythm. And then I write every poetic song down to an instrumental, leaving them imprinted like tattooed scars reminding me that there is a liberatory groove I was riding to and a marching beat I am out to drum. Of course, I still like, want, and need. I'm no rarity in that way. I, too, beg for "Easy 1977," like the year my sister was born, so I can sing it like "I'm easy like Sunday morning" and wish for all the things I want, like capitalism sneakin' a ride in the back pocket. All the things I was, all the things I've been through, and all the things I have left to do are still right here. From time to time, I shelve them and leave them tucked away in their sleeves, especially when I am not ready to listen to them or when I don't want to remember. But I do, every now and then, if the moment calls to me, pull out one and let it gleam around the twelves and tell me about a battle or two while I sit with the pain from hearing that joint with a slow head nod—hands in the air and everything. Towards that almighty sky.

I don't think I'll ever have that closure in a book fairytale or find some kind of epiphany out of this battle. My father certainly didn't give me all the answers. I will never know what he went through or how he suffered. I will never know the father he would have been to me or who he was striving to be. I still live with the hurt and pain, as I still love and cherish what good we had. And I suppose these grey areas leave me being okay with never knowing what lies ahead of me or never knowing which opponent is next. I did, however, stop competing, as my last DJ battle was in 2001. But if there's anything I've learned from competing, it's that perhaps it isn't really a fight. Perhaps it's more of a surrender. Surrender to whatever may come, surrender to the opponent who may leave me skippin' records on those tables, to another heart surgery or maybe another love loss. Surrender to the battle and trust that whatever it may be, or whatever it may look like, that it will leave me with a crate full of records to play. After all, there's a movement I've been counting on, a beat I've been searching for, a poetic song I have yet to write, and a battle I'm always ready to face.

César Ramon García was born and raised in San Diego and has overcome many obstacles that once hindered him from progressing in life. He has been a long-time advocate on social justice issues that have impacted him and his community. He hopes to make a difference by being a voice for those who haven't found their own. César's goal is to help others find their passion for the betterment of our society.

César Ramon García
The Long Walk: Or, Childhood Derailed

I want to dedicate this story to children who don't have a voice to share what they have been through or what they might be currently experiencing. I also dedicate it to those many people who have found themselves in prisons and institutions because they haven't been able to process their horrible realities.

Looking back at my childhood, I can't recall any moments that were truly pleasant. If there were any, they were pushed aside by instances of chaos. I remember shattered dishes and violent expressions of control. I cannot forget the many times that police officers came to take my dad away in handcuffs, or that person who appeared friendly but was only out to fulfill his disgusting habits. This was my childhood and it haunted me even though I tried my hardest to escape it.

Fuck this shit! As I ran out of the house, all I could hear was, "César, you have to go to school!" I was tired of listening to my mom complain about me ditching class. I was running away and headed to the forbidden land, my father's house, whether she knew it or not. She seemed to think that because I wore old clothes and fake Nikes, these were the reasons for my rebellion. Did she really believe that lack of material possessions had led me astray? Or that moving constantly from one place to another had made it any easier for me to fit in? Shit, I was upset about some things, but out-of-date clothes and changing schools were the least of my problems.

So I decided to go where my mom told me never to go again.

I was on my way to see my father. How I would get there is a story all in itself. At the time I ran away, I was a student at Granger Middle School in National City where I lived on the cusp of Paradise Hills. The path I took led me to a dirt road that was nestled between Rachel and Van Ness Avenue. On that day I wore bright-colored baggy clothes with shell-toe Adidas, so being discreet was going to be hard. My first thought was to find a way to stay incognito from my mother in case she was out looking for me. The journey ahead of me was four miles, but I didn't see this as an obstacle because I was determined to see my father. I walked a fine line between two avenues, between two hoods, and between two parents who were slowly starting to lose me. The dirt road was long behind me, and now I was trekking west on 18th street headed towards the infamous Highland Avenue. As I walked, the only person I could think of was my father and his reaction when I showed up at his doorstep. I had a feeling that he would be surprised to see me. The last time I had seen him was when I had played little league at Memorial Park. During those visits at the park, my parents' marriage was already over. The communication between us was non-existent, but he had made it a habit to watch me play every now and then. My mother told my coach that I wasn't allowed to talk to my dad. He knew his boundaries, and I knew mine.

I remember a particular time at the park when he came to watch me.

As I positioned myself in the batter's box, my father stood behind the backstop. I was a bit nervous, but I wasn't fearful. I was mentally prepared as I waited for the pitcher's next move, the wind up, a swing and a miss. My father said, "César, keep your eye on the ball and wait for your pitch." My father was coaching a son that never looked at him to acknowledge his presence.

The little league memory began to fade as I continued down Highland Avenue. The feelings of freedom started to take over, and I was reminded again of the journey I had ahead of me. I noticed the cars and all the businesses that were open to the public. As I went past Wells Fargo, I looked at Price Breakers and then glanced at LA Rack. When I finally got to Plaza Boulevard, my tummy started to feel empty. Maybe it was the Burger King that sparked my hunger. I had no money, so I went to the 7-Eleven on Eighth Street and put some candy in my pocket.

The store attendant gave me a weird look as if to say that he knew what I had done, but it didn't faze me. I just kept going. That's when I remembered one of my parents' domestic disputes.

He kicked in the door and started to beat on my mother. His words were as violent as the fists he swung at her. That's how he reminded her who wore the pants in the family. I stayed on my bunk bed with the pillow over my head covering my ears. The only time I looked into the living room was to see if he had finally stopped, but I wish I hadn't. My mother was laid out on the floor as he kicked her stomach repeatedly.

As I snapped back from that memory, I started to envision just how happy my father would be to see me. I had to motivate myself because I was beginning to get tired of walking. Up until that point I hadn't paid much attention to people on the street. I was far more focused on the cars that passed me bumping really loud music. It was like I was invisible to the world. I was a teenage boy in search of his father. I didn't stop to talk to anyone because I didn't trust adults. They were unpredictable, and they always made me feel scared and uncomfortable. Especially adult males because they grossed me the fuck out. I definitely didn't make eye contact with any of them as I continued on my mission. Anything to escape that reality because I was in constant fear of memories like this:

I was only seven when my dad's friend came to my house after my mother and father had just finished fighting. I was really scared because my mom was bleeding a lot. My father greeted him like nothing was wrong. My father's friend asked if he could take me to the park, so we could play soccer. The next thing I knew, I was in a car headed to the park, but we never got there. Instead we went to his house, and he asked if I was hungry. He made a sandwich for me, but after I ate my food, things got weird. I never knew any-

thing about the things introduced to me that day. No one had ever touched me like that except for my mom when I was taking a bath as a child. It made me uneasy and uncomfortable. I had no idea what was going on.

That memory went away as I was walking out of the city limits of National City. Highland Avenue turned into 47th Street. I passed by the drive-through liquor store that has a purple cow on the rooftop. As I walked up the hill, the 805 South onramp was on my left. I had finally stepped out of National City and was now on the street that winds through Shelltown, a neighborhood of San Diego. The parking lot to the Victory Outreach was packed. I was excited to be outside of his house because now I could finally tell him how much I missed him. I walked up the steps and knocked on his door. It took some time for him to finally answer, but when he did, he wasn't too thrilled to see me. He invited me in and directed me to the sofa. He went to the bigger couch and quickly fell asleep. I sat forever waiting for him to wake up. I began to think that something was wrong with him because he slept for a long time.

Empty beer cans were scattered across the living room. The air smelled stale of dirty feet and alcoholic perspiration. My father was in a deep sleep. I was wide-awake with the excitement of finally being with him. An overdramatic couple argued on the television set. Novelas bored me, and I was reminded of my mother. After I had sat there for hours, he finally got up, asked me about my mom, then asked how I had gotten there.

She wasn't too happy that I had gone to see him, but she came and got me anyway. On the ride back, she told me that visiting him could only make the situation worse. Up until that point, all I wanted was to see my father and to have him in my life. I had never thought that his leaving would be so permanent. The scars that my father and his friend left were enough to derail my development as a child.

I sought help in professional therapy, and by doing so I learned how to trust others. The events from my past no longer haunt me today, and through the process of self-help I began to forgive my father for being so absent in my life. I let go of those experiences that led me down the road of shame and self-doubt, because it was this path that hindered my personal growth. It caused me to think I wasn't worthy of having good relationships. I know now that what happened to me was innocent on my part but immoral for someone else. Resilience and deep self-reflection have taught me so, and I have learned so much. If I could have understood then what I understand now, I would have just said, "Dad, please don't leave me."

Mariah Jameson is a community activist, academic achiever, and mother of two. Although 13 years of her childhood were spent in the foster care system, Mariah has never allowed her past to dictate her future. She was born and raised in Southeast San Diego and graduated from Lincoln High School. She is currently enrolled at San Diego City College where she serves as the Umoja Club President.

Mariah Jameson
Foster Kid

Dedicated to my children, Saniah and Josiah, for bringing light to all my dark days. And to the children of the foster care system, regardless of how your story begins, you have the power to choose your ending.

My brother Isiah and I had been in the house alone for three days without her, and by the third day we had finished off all of the bread and milk, so we had nothing left to eat. My mom often left us alone, and this time it had gone from a few hours to a few days. Isiah looked at me and said, "I'm going to the store to get us some noodles or something. Lock the door behind me and don't let anyone in the house." We had been eating bread with butter and sugar for so long that I didn't even realize it could ever run out. Isiah left the house and I locked the door. Thirty minutes later he came back from the store with some apples, a couple of packs of noodles, and a loaf of bread. All of this he had stuffed in his jacket sleeve. He did this every time my mom left us without enough food. He didn't care or even think to care of the risks he took. He just knew he had to feed us.

Since I was so young, only 5 at the time, I didn't realize the severity of the situation. My brother, who was only 7 years old at the time, was often left as my caretaker, making sure I ate, walking me to school, helping me with my homework, etcetera. All of this, and he was only two years older than me. My mother's addiction to drugs and money took priority over her children. She had 6 kids and wasn't able to take care of any of us. My two oldest and youngest siblings were already living with other family members. A few weeks after one of the last times she had left us alone for days, we were staying with my aunt and her two boys when my brother and I were taken into foster care by a social worker.

My first visit with my brother after being separated was for my sixth birthday. My social worker brought him to my foster mom's house, and we left for McDonald's together in her car. Before leaving the house, my foster mom took a picture of me and my brother in front of her big fish tank. I remember my brother couldn't stop smiling like he had a surprise for me. I didn't care what it was I was just so happy to see him. He even looked taller.

When we made it to McDonald's, the surprise he had for me was sitting at a table near the play gym. It was my mom. I hadn't seen her in two months. The day the police had come and gotten us from my aunt's house, she had left us there for two weeks with no call or anything. I didn't think we would ever see her again.

"What is she doing here?" His smile left his face as soon as he saw the anger on mine. "She's going to get us back, Ry. We won't have to be in those homes anymore." My brother couldn't help it. He believed my mom could do no wrong, but even though I was younger than him, I had grown not to trust anything she said. My social worker must've known I wasn't too happy about my mom being there because she quickly reassured me if I wanted her to leave she would have my mom's case manager take her home. "Come on, Ry, just talk to her," my brother begged.

See, my brother and I were supposed to have scheduled visits with my mom every weekend, but my mom showed up to visits whenever she felt like it. Sometimes our visits were at McDonald's, and sometimes we met with her at this place with a lot of toys, but every visit was supervised and only for a few hours.

The months to come were a wave of emotions. "She isn't coming," I thought to myself. We had been at the visiting place for an hour, and nothing. I knew this was going to happen. I knew she wasn't coming. This was the third visit in a row she would miss.

"Can we leave now?" I asked.

"You don't want to wait a few more minutes, Mariah? She might come," my social worker responded.

I walked away from the dolls I was playing with and kicked at the ground. I turned away from her, so she wouldn't see me cry.

"No, I want to leave. I'm ready to go now."

She could hear it in my voice even though she couldn't see my tears.

"I am sorry, Mariah. Maybe next weekend she will come," my social worker said. "You know she is trying. Don't give up on her."

I stood in silence with tears streaming down my face. My mom hadn't shown up for our last three visits, and she wouldn't be showing up for any more. I knew it and my social worker knew it. My brother Isiah walked into the room from the bathroom, and before even seeing my face he knew it, too.

"Maybe next visit…." he began, putting his jacket on and walking towards me. "Let's go, Riah. Put your jacket on."

Months went by, and we still hadn't seen or heard from my mom. Each weekend she didn't show up only meant one thing to me: She didn't care about us, and she was never getting us back. By this time, I had been in only one foster home, but now my social worker had an ulterior motive. She was trying to convince me to get adopted. I knew this meant I would get a new family, and my brother wasn't coming with me. So I told her no each time she brought it up. There was no way I was going anywhere else without him. I was already only able to see him on the weekends, and adoption to me meant not seeing him ever again.

My social worker came to visit me one day out of the blue. I say "out of the blue" because I expected her on the weekends only, so for her to come to visit me on a Wednesday was rare. She had a peculiar look on her face when she saw me. That could only mean one thing to me: She was up to something.

"Mariah, there is something important we have to talk about today. Something I need you to understand." She began moving her folder and purse out of the way to sit closer to me. "Your mom has lost her rights to you and your brother. You are now a ward of the state. This means that I must make the best decision for you. No matter what you want."

"My mom isn't getting me back?" I asked.

"As of now, no. She has to do some things to try but, ultimately, she probably won't."

I gazed down at the floor for a while before she interrupted my thoughts. My mom wasn't getting me back…mom wasn't getting me back?

"Do you want to be on the news, Mariah? There's a special called Adopt 8. It will help us find a family for you." Adopt 8 was a special feature on channel 8.

"I don't want a family."

"Mariah, as of now, you need one. I am going to get you adopted. Everything will be fine, okay?" She gathered up her things and called for my foster mom. I could hear them whispering about the news thing and then she left. It was as if nothing I said mattered anymore. No one cared about my thoughts or where I wanted to be. All they wanted to do was take me away from my brother and send me with some family…again.

That week I did the Adopt 8 special. The news lady talked to me as I played in the playground and rollerbladed down the sidewalk. It wasn't long after it aired that my social worker received notice of a potential family that wanted me. It also wasn't long after it aired that I realized my brother and I would never be together again.

I left my first foster home a month after the Adopt 8 special had aired and moved in with my new family. The first weekend I was with them, they took me to Disneyland. It was like a dream. I had never been to

Disneyland before, only seen it on TV, so of course I was happy. What 8-year-old wouldn't be? Living with this family was ideal. They were black, well off, and had one son. They just needed a daughter to complete their household, and they thought the little black girl roller blading in the park was it. The first time I knew I wasn't it, I got in trouble for talking back. I was told to go to my room; there would be no dinner for me that night. The next time I got in trouble for talking in class, I was slapped. A few months went by before the next incident, and then my "mom" choked me and made me stay in my room for a day. By this time, I had been told I wasn't allowed to call my brother anymore, and that's when I decided I couldn't be there any longer. The next day at school I pushed a girl down and jumped on top of her, punching her and yelling. I got suspended from school and sent to bed with no dinner. When I woke up the next morning my "dad" told me to get in the car. He drove me straight to the county office with a box. He left me at the front door of the county building with my belongings in a box and drove off. I would never let anyone try to adopt me again after that.

I spent the next thirteen years of my life going from foster home to foster home. Thirteen different families, but the abuse never stopped, and I never told anyone. I pretended I was someone else with each move, because each time I had new parents and new siblings. No one knew the truth about me, and no one would know unless I told them. I had a new identity every time I changed schools and an answer for every question my new friends asked. Each time I moved, the resentment I had developed for my mom was projected onto my new "mom." I called each foster mom by their first name, and they hated that. This would eventually cause animosity between us, and then the physical abuse would start. I lived in only two homes where I was never harmed: the very first foster home and the last.

Often, I think back to that first visit at McDonald's with my mom and brother. Walking towards my mom felt like I was walking down the longest road ever. Everything surrounding us in McDonald's froze, and it became silent. My stomach dropped as if I was flying down a large, steep hill at high speeds. I was going to tell my mom how I really felt about her. I wanted to tell her how much it hurt to be abandoned. That was all until she got up and ran towards me with her arms open wide, scooping my little tiny frame off the ground, all while crying and saying, " I am so sorry, Ry Ry, I'm going to do whatever it takes to get you back." I didn't say any of the things I needed to say to her. I didn't stand up for myself or my brother that day. Instead I cried like the little six-year-old that I was. I cried to my mommy and told her how much I missed her.

Photo: Stephen Alberts

David was born and raised by a single mother with five kids in San Diego where he grew up disenfranchised with no guidance and few resources. Inevitably, he succumbed to his circumstances and was made a ward of the state at an early age. He stayed on probation until he was a young adult. Through the love and grace of God, and motivation from his daughter, he escaped the systemic traps and overcame the challenges to write a new story. A narrative that doesn't include bars.

David Grant
It Wasn't Supposed to Be Like This

To those who navigate the treacherous waters with no compass or
light and struggle to hold it together. To those who, aware of the
risk, cast your net into the night's storm wholeheartedly with the
hopes of providing for your family. And to my daughter, Cecilia,
who saved my life.

"Mr. Grant, if you don't open the door, we will force our way in." It was at this moment that I thought to myself: it wasn't supposed to be like this. I could tell from the tone in their voices that I was going to jail and that there was no way out of this hot situation. I can still see the officers in every window of my apartment with their guns drawn and red beams blazing through as though my residence were some kind of militarized fortress that had harbored some kind of dangerous fugitive. I had two decisions to make, follow the hostile commands of the officers outside and come out, or not comply and make them come in and get me. Since I already mistrusted "peace officers" from prior experiences growing up, one which resulted in me being shot with a Taser, I decided it'd be best if I just lie down on my bed to avoid any discrepancy. From the Southeast to the South Bay, and being black and Mexican, I had grown up with a firm understanding of how law enforcement functioned and treated those in my communities. Many times, they abused their authority and detached from the realities of those suffering in the community. They showed little to no empathy, all while operating in a militarized fashion. I didn't want to be shot again, or possibly slammed coming out of my residence, so I thought it'd be best if I just stayed there on the bed and allowed them to do their job. Boy, was I wrong. If I had known then what I know now, I believe I would have just come out as they commanded. Unfortunately, sometimes in life we act on emotions as opposed to logic and end up learning things the hard way.

I was laid out on my bed, and as I heard them kick in the front door, I sat up and threw out the blunt that I was smoking into the sink. I figured since I was going to jail, I might as well be high before I was handcuffed in shackles and hauled away. This was a good indication of the state of mind that often fueled my ego. The years of neglect I felt from being in the system consumed me and calcified my heart to the point that my spirit was in a constant state of "fuck it," and every time something extreme happened, or when the ground shifted from under me, any turbulence, I learned to embrace it. My shoulder had just been rebuilt from years of fighting in the streets, and I had spent my whole life in survival mode. Any time I was called out, or felt someone attempting to punk me, I immediately "threw on the riders" and welcomed the funk, so to speak. This was how I operated, as a means to survive and vent my frustrations. So one can understand that when the young deputy made a threatening remark towards me, like the flip of a switch, it was enough for me to turn off that voice of reason and not comply.

As I heard them gain access through the front door of my residence, I locked my hands together assuming the position that felt all so familiar, thinking to myself, "Here we go again." I had no clue that they would be sending in their Gestapo, and by that I mean their police dog. As they kicked in my bedroom door, there I lay like an idiot, exposed and vulnerable, just waiting for this K9 to rip into my flesh, and as he did, I remember screaming in agony. With the exception of my shoulder reconstruction surgery a few months prior, I can't remember there ever being a more excruciating and immediate sense of physical pain in my life. There is nothing that can describe the trauma of an animal ripping into your flesh. After the German shepherd was finished taking a bite out of crime, it released its grasp, and what felt like an eternity was now over. As I was cuffed, a female officer was examining my 300-pound old-school safe that was tucked away in my closet, and all I could focus on in disbelief was the latch that was pointed upright, leaving my safe unlocked. As I heard one of the deputies call for another in excitement like they had just hit the jackpot, my heart dropped and all I can remember thinking was "This shit just isn't right." They found the pound of marijuana and ledger, along with money in the safe, everything a prosecutor would need to put me away for three to five years. Because of the overwhelming evidence, I ended up doing what most young men who are railroaded by the system and have no resources do, and that's take the plea deal offered by the DA. I was away for about a year, which was the longest year of my life, and as I sat in my cell, I couldn't help but think that I had spent my whole life avoiding gangs and dodging other obstacles in the hood, and yet there I sat like so many I grew up with. All because I desperately wanted to provide for my daughter and give her everything I didn't have growing up.

But it wasn't supposed to be like this.

I remember long walks to school in first grade with my older brother. Walks that seemed endless, just to get to and from school. I'm sure it wasn't more than a few city blocks, but at that age, the world was immense. I wore hand-me-down shoes given to me by my foster mother and I remember my feet hurt from the blisters caused by all the walking. "Come on, David, let's run away," my brother would say as we walked home from school, and as much as I didn't want to walk back into our reality, which was our foster home, I still couldn't find the courage to break away. From my small, child's vantage point, the world was a frightening place filled with hostility, chaos, and overflowing with neglect.

I went to Johnson Elementary where many like myself felt the effects that addiction and the war on drugs had on our community, an era when D.A.R.E officers visited with stickers and gave talks at elementary schools about growing up healthy as they locked up our fathers, mothers, brothers, and sisters for possession, leaving us to navigate the treacherous system without guidance. This was right after the failed policies of the Reagan years and Iran–Contra where drugs were smuggled into the country in high volumes assisted by the government and then funneled into communities like mine. And, as if that weren't enough, during this time few or no resources were directed to our communities to counter or combat the addiction. In fact, I can remember my only uncle making America's Most Wanted for drug manufacturing when actually the DEA supplied all the chemicals needed to manufacture the poison that has continued to plague my family. My only uncle, the man who taught me how to be a man and work with my hands, was hauled off for nine years; and when we needed doctors and shrinks in our community, we received chemicals and sentences.

My parents were plagued by addiction and were in an abusive relationship, so my three siblings and I were removed by the state and held in the Polanski Center. It was a facility that housed neglected children, the first time I experienced institutionalization. This facility honestly felt like baby jail. In fact, it's the first time I was thrown in with a homogenous group of disenfranchised youth and left to fend for myself. We were all in the same boat with a few things in common, which was the unfortunate cargo of abuse and neglect that each of us carried, and the weight of it all was so heavy. I can distinctly remember we weren't able to move freely around the facility. Yup, this was the first time I experienced confinement. There was something unnatural about being a child with the inability to move about freely: unable to run outside, no freedom to express myself, and often punished for no reason.

I see now that I was being groomed in some sense. The staff were really guards; the facility was the institution; and their so-called "rec time" was in fact yard time. For as long as I can remember, I've been a product of the system—always bound and institutionalized, in some sense, by the state. From juvenile hall, which was a jail for adolescents, to Campo where I slaved away shoveling dirt and filling sand bags to receive a lighter sentence, there wasn't ever a time when I didn't feel commoditized or used as a pawn by the state. All I desperately sought and longed for was a stable home, a safe place I could shelter and anchor, free from the troubles and stresses of the world. I remember the turbulence from change and neglect, the constant shifting and feeling of never really belonging, and as I sat in my cell awaiting trial, all these feelings came rushing back.

It wasn't supposed to be this way, but this was the space I occupied. I always said if there were a market for oranges in the hood then I would have sold those. So from 2004 to 2008 I worked for countless companies installing tile floors. I had developed a skill from my uncle, setting tile, and after I found myself homeless at sixteen, I was able to maintain and survive working on my hands and knees. But when the housing market crashed in 2008, tile work became scarce, as many lost their homes. I needed to make more money, as I now had a newborn to feed and a wife to support. I went from doing remodels every week to every other week to not at all. Because the people in my diverse little world smoked marijuana, it just made more sense to provide my neighbors who depended on marijuana for its medicinal properties a better alternative than opioids. In fact, many of my neighbors were elderly conservatives, who would otherwise continue to experience long bouts of pain.

We often judge others, never really understanding that we as human beings are all products of our environment, bounded by limitations. That is not to justify my decisions, rather to rationalize and help some understand why I made the decisions I made. Two years prior to this incident, I had just reconnected with my father who'd been absent most of my life, and shortly after our reunion he died of a heart attack. To lose him so abruptly left me feeling empty. So when the housing market crashed, and employment was scarce, I desperately needed to keep my family intact, and my options were limited. When I married and started my family, I felt as though I was complete, and I was willing to do whatever it took to keep it that way, and now here I was lying on this hospital bed being treated for a K9 bite, headed to George Bailey Detention Facility. And in a blink of an eye, everything that I had worked so hard to build was all gone. Everything.

You see, it wasn't supposed to be like this.

Kirin earned a Master of Social Work and Nonprofit Administration degree from San Diego State University, where she learned the challenges she saw in her community growing up could be turned into sources of strength. She is a wife, teacher, and proud mama to two young boys.

Kirin Macapugay

Paradise Hills, 1994

I dedicate this story to my ancestors, who sit on my left shoulder, to my parents, who taught me to hold tight to my roots, to the rest of my family and friends, who serve as my lighthouse, to my husband and sons, who serve as my anchor, and to the people of Paradise Hills. You can't know where you're going until you remember where you've been. All love.

I grew up during an era of high gang violence and activity in a Southeast San Diego neighborhood known as Paradise Hills, just a few minutes north of the Mexican border and east of the US Naval Base. Much is known and documented about black and Mexican gangs, but there are only a few firsthand accounts of Asian gangs in the area at the time. Their increasing activity led to a special gang division in the San Diego Police Department (SDPD). Filipino and other Asian police officers were tasked with working with identified gang members and at-risk youth.

When I was 13, I started dating a boy who was in a gang, one with roots in the Philippines. I remember sitting in this friend's living room, his dad warning us about being obvious when engaging in certain activities—how law enforcement in the United States was not as easily "bought off" like it was in his hometown in the Philippines.

For the next few years, I flitted in and out of different relationships and different groups, from actual gangs to graffiti and breakdancing crews. But we knew who was in a gang and who was not. The lines were clear. Being around gang members did not automatically make you one. Everyone wore baggy jeans and crisp white Hanes t-shirts, but we knew the differences in flannel shirts and bandanas. To be a gang member, there were rites of passage you needed to have gone through. Rites involving fists, or worse.

One Friday evening in 1994, a group of my friends and I—five girls and three boys—were getting into our cars outside of my neighbor's house. We had only met at the house to share rides. It was a mutual meeting spot. I noticed a car pull up across the street but did not pay it any mind. Then I saw the tall lanky boy walking towards us.

He was Filipino, like us, so I thought maybe he was a friend of my friends. Then I saw the gun in his hand, cocked sideways like he probably saw in some movie. He aimed the gun at us. It was the first time I had seen a gun pointed at me. I don't remember him saying anything. The silence is what made it more absurd. He didn't ask who we were. It was as if he knew us and deliberately targeted us, but none of us recognized him.

I ran. I ran before I could make sense of what was happening. I ran fearing he might have followed me. I crouched behind my dad's old van, hoping he couldn't hear me breathe—

In that moment I recalled months earlier when I had stood at a National City cemetery, tears falling into the grass. Many of us watched as they lowered my friend's casket into the ground. We were fifteen years old then. It was the third friend I had had to bury since adolescence.

Now I heard my heartbeat as I crouched behind that van, and then I thought, "Am I next?"

Suddenly it was quiet. Then I heard the crying. I ran out to the front yard and saw my friend on the ground, bleeding. We dragged him into the living room where my auntie started wailing and screaming, his blood seeping into the carpet. But he was alive. We were all alive. The news crews and the police arrived. The spinning lights from the top of the cop cars blended with the red lights on the cameras. It was all lights and sirens and voices. His mom and sisters arrived. I brought them to my living room and watched them weep on the couch, holding each other rocking. I did my best to tell them it would be okay. I heard my words float out of my mouth, but I didn't really know what they meant because I couldn't understand how this had happened to us and my neighborhood—to my community—so many, many times.

A few days after the shooting, we were each individually interviewed by a police officer. I clearly remember being pulled out of class by the plainclothes officer, and how I thought he would be more empathetic being a Filipino investigator. Instead, his line of questioning made me feel like I was being interrogated as a suspect, rather than being a victim. He asked me if we were in a gang, and I said no. He asked what we were doing outside (like that was illegal), and I told him we were all about to leave. He kept asking me over and over, "Is there something you're not telling me?" as if I were lying. He never asked how my friends and I were. Days later he came to my friend's house who had been hit by the ricocheting bullet, showed us photos of potential suspects, and asked if any of them looked like the shooter. None of them did, and that was the last we heard about that investigation.

I was 16 then. I would experience another shooting incident in National City in 2003. It was minor in that it was a pellet gun, though it shattered my window while I was driving my old pickup truck. I remember standing along the road with NCPD, who told me they had had a slew of similar incidents on that street—the ramp off the 805 coming into Palm Avenue that thousands of people take every day. To this day I don't know if anyone was ever arrested for either shooting.

At the time, shootings like this were just part of life. It was not until I attended San Diego State University and met more people from outside of the South Bay and San Diego that I realized the circumstances I grew up in were *not* normal, were *not* the average. I had buried someone I knew and cared about every year of my life since I had been 11 years old. In college, some of my counterparts had never been to a funeral, while I had already grown familiar with loss. It was then I began to question why this was the case.

I originally majored in psychology, thinking issues like this were unique to individuals and that things like gang activity, violence, and drug abuse were solely personal. Then I learned about social work. I learned about community organizing, systemic theories, macro practice, and I learned about trends in communities. I learned about lack of opportunity, lack of resources, how hard it is to expect people to do well when they have not been given the education, the knowledge, or the resources.

More importantly, I learned things did not have to be the way they were. Since then, I have dedicated myself to grassroots-based change and policy advocacy. I sit at tables of people who make decisions on the kinds of resources our communities need and the kinds of laws affecting our families. Many times I am the only woman, or the only person of color, or the only individual who grew up with these kinds of experiences.

Many of the guys I know from "back in the day" who got "caught up" in gang life are out of prison now. They went in as boys and are out as men who need to rediscover how to survive. They have found ways to live and to still have families. Some of them choose to give back and make sure other kids don't have to grow up with what we did. Now that I have children of my own, I pray they will never know what it's like to have to stare down or run from another young person who looks like them. Even today, when I think about that young man, I do not feel hate, or resentment. I wish I could sit with him, talk to him about how we should move on from there, and tell him loud bangs still make me jump. I want to tell him he can still turn things around, reach back to pull up young men caught up in the same shit he was back then.

Darius Spearman is a husband, father, educator, and author of *Between the Color Lines: A History of African Americans on the California Frontier from 1769 Through Reconstruction*. He was awarded a Master of Arts degree in history (2000) and education (2006) and joined the faculty of the Department of Black Studies at San Diego City College in 2007.

Darius Spearman

This Film Is Not Yet Rated....

> *I dedicate this story to my wife and everyone else who loved me
> unconditionally and without judgment. It is also a big "FUCK
> YOU!" to everyone who thought my success an impossibility. My
> success is just as much a product of love on the part of those who
> saw past my circumstances as it is an act of raw defiance on my part
> toward those who wrote me off.*

I remember being told once that my life would make for a great movie. I
don't know about that. The comment did get me to thinking, though. If
my life were made into a movie, which studio would pick up the distribu-
tion rights? Would my story be the Disney studio production of a homeless first-generation college student who defied the odds on his way to an
honors degree, *cum laude*, with distinction from my department and two
master's degrees? The inspirational story that taps into the heartwarming
and often-peddled narrative that if you just work hard enough you too
can achieve your dreams? Or would it be picked up by the San Diego-
based pornography production company *Naughty America*? The story
of a "barely 18" homeless teenager with a talent for dance who avoided
sleeping on the streets by frequenting the sleaziest night clubs and going
home with the first woman to approach? Those are both my movie. The
script depends on the particular lens the director chooses to draw into
focus. Whatever narrative emerges is a choice I leave to the reader. This
film is not yet rated....

Act 1

Regardless of the narrative, most of the story points converge on a single moment—my high school graduation. As I stood in the middle of the stage, shaking hands with my high school principal, and accepting my diploma while smiling broadly in my blue graduation robe, my smile belied a cold, hard fact. I had no idea where I was going next. The recession of 1990–1992 had hit the real estate market hard. My mother, who was a real estate agent, told me midway through my senior year that I would have find another place to live.

I wasn't penniless. I did have a part-time job and at one point worked seven days a week shortly after graduation, yet I was still homeless. It turns out it is extremely expensive to be poor. When one has no refrigerator, fast food becomes an expensive staple. With no permanent address, registering an automobile becomes a logistical tap dance. The state's remedy typically requires an appearance before a judge to pay a fine, but to what address is the notice to appear sent? When one fails to appear in court, a $30 fine can balloon into hundreds of dollars. The three months rent I needed in order to secure housing (first month, last month, and deposit) thus remained out of reach.

My choices were harsh, but all were carefully calculated. Gas or food? Usually gas won. I can go without food for a couple of days, but without gas I could not maintain employment and was without any income at all. Besides, at the restaurant where I bussed tables I could get at least one meal per shift.

My first two semesters in college were a flop. I had no idea what I was doing. All I knew was that I didn't want to be poor for the rest of my life, so I kept at it. Fear? That was also a choice—a calculated one. I had no time for fear. Besides, I had already fallen just about as far as one could fall. What did I have to fear at this point? I weighed nearly 100 pounds less than I do now, but I don't remember ever feeling hungry. I suppose that, too, was a choice.

In spite of the popular notion that poor people are drug-addicted moochers unworthy of our collective concern, I had stayed away from drugs and alcohol, even though my very first memory in life at about two years old is of my parents getting high in front of me. I was making good choices, working hard, taking personal responsibility, and pulling myself up by my bootstraps. That's the Disney version of this phase of my life, not an untrue version of events but also not the entire story. So before pitching that story, before using me as the model that poor folks should emulate, there are a few more details the reader should know.

Act 2

I didn't have much in the way of bootstraps to pull on, but I did have good friends. My closest friends and I at the time, Journey L, Mayhem, DJ Shaboo, and Tupac, were all either dancers, aspiring hip-hop artists or both. Tupac, whose living situation was similar to mine, stayed down the street on the couch of DJ Shaboo. Tupac, of course would later go on to solo fame, but he began as a stage dancer for the local hip-hop group Digital Underground. By the time his solo career took off with songs like "Keep Ya Head Up" and "Dear Mama," Tupac had a major falling out with me and the other folks in our group, but that is another story unto itself—a deleted scene that shall, for the moment, be best left on the cutting room floor.

I was the quietest one in the group. Journey L was the flirt. It was at his pad that I crashed during my last six months of high school. Shaboo was the craziest, most spontaneous, and most unpredictable in the group. He was also a jokester who would say absolutely anything and everything in order to embarrass the living shit out of whoever happened to be his target of the moment. In one such moment we were all crammed into my 1973 Ford Maverick driving along the 101 freeway when he spotted a random car full of young twentysomething women. When my car happened to come alongside theirs, he suddenly rolled down his window and shouted over to them, "HEEEEYYY.... HE WANNA LICK YO PUSSY!!!" My initial shock turned to absolute horror when I looked over to find him pointing directly and emphatically at me.

Mayhem was my closest friend in high school. We were so inseparable that the sight of me without Mayhem usually prompted an immediate query from Shaboo. "Where's Black-ass at?" Mayhem was usually close behind and within earshot, which typically resulted in a quick comeback and a round of "yo mama" jokes.

Tupac was the most lighthearted of the group—the complete alter ego to the thug life persona he would become famous for. I remember every encounter I have ever had with Tupac the same way, his broad smile full of teeth from ear to ear along with a hearty embrace. Although the scene seems a bit chaotic, these are the folks who got me through that initial six months and across the Tamalpais High School graduation stage.

We looked out for each other. I always knew that if any of my friends had a roof over his head I had a place to sleep, even if it was only a couch. We shared most of what we had, but in order to have anything to share in terms of food or basic necessities I had to be a bit more creative. My limited options were all carefully calculated. I worked out a system. Large items: bread, crackers and the like would go into my shopping basket. I stood in line, my items were rung up, I paid, smiled (sometimes flirtatiously) got my receipt and walked out of the store. Other items: lunch meat, canned sardines and anything else that was small enough walked out of the store in my pockets. If I was ever caught and apprehended, then at least the problem of my food and housing would be solved. Calculated.

For me, the calculation had little to do with the morality of my choices. It was simply a matter of pragmatism. For some moviegoers, however, this part of the story might be a hard sell. The popular narrative of the 1990s frames poverty not so much as an economic state but as a character deficit. After all, as the French poet Anatole France observed over a century ago, "The law, in its majestic equality, forbids the rich as well as the poor to sleep under bridges, to beg in the streets, and to steal bread."

After a few months, the twins who were listed as the tenants of the Section 8 housing unit where I stayed moved out. Because of the long Section 8 waiting list, we couldn't simply slide in, so we faced eviction. My home then became my 1973 Ford Maverick. During that time, however, I acquired some skills that would become critically important during this phase of my story.

When I wasn't working or studying, I spent much of my time clubbing with my friends. I had honed my dance style and moved on to some amateur work as a dancer for *Friday Night Live* and some low paying gigs as a stage dancer for a small Bay Area record company. Of all of my friends, I was the most shy when it came to talking to women. I skipped my high school prom ostensibly because I couldn't afford a tux. At least that was the story I presented. It wasn't a lie, but it masked a more underlying truth. I couldn't get a date. Pick-up lines were not my forte, and I was never any good at "spittin' game." Oddly enough, though, this is the exact moment where the story turns into a porno flick [cue cheesy 70s jazz music]. I didn't attend my prom, but I didn't exactly spend prom night at home alone....

In the nightclub I was in my element. With the lights dim and the "Humpty Dance" blaring in the background, my confidence as a dancer more than compensated for the confidence I lacked when it came to verbal wit. In that arena, my particular combination of hip-hop, jazz isolations and body rolls were all the communication I needed.

I was so used to being rejected in high school that at first it was hard for me to get used to all the attention I was receiving. I wasn't even trying. The very thing that in every other setting had been my biggest liability had become, in that space, my biggest asset—simply being my authentic self in my own body doing what I enjoyed doing. Consequently, at

Baxter's, which was well known throughout the area as a hook-up spot for folks looking for one-nighters, I always left with someone without having to do much talking. Usually that someone was close to twice my age. These encounters became my secret life that few people knew about. After graduation it became a way of life and an alternative to sleeping in my car.

Because I was never the type of person who could end a relationship on a sour note, it wasn't long before I developed a fairly wide circle of "friends" (with benefits) before the term became popular. They were, in fact, genuinely friends, and I remember them being very good to me. In return, to the women who took me in and showed me love at a time when I had nothing, I was fiercely loyal. At the same time, there was a peculiar sense of detachment and an understanding that when the encounter was over, we would each do our own thing. There was never any jealousy on anyone's part. I suppose because there was no real sense of attachment. There was complete honesty in each of these encounters, but simultaneously there was nothing resembling any real intimacy.

Before long, my circle of friends and I began to frequent another venue, club Bedroxx. As the name would imply, Bedroxx had a reputation as a meat market that far exceeded that of Baxter's. Although smaller, this scene featured something that Baxter's did not—female strippers Wednesday nights, male strippers Thursday nights. One night a dancer known by the moniker "Hot Chocolate" struck up a conversation about how much money he made performing on Thursday nights. Before I knew it, the emcee, Jo Jo, had signed me up to perform the next Thursday. Jo Jo, often referred to as the biggest flirt in the county, was an amazing jazz dancer who was advanced in years but still had a few signature moves that I couldn't keep up with. Thus, by age eighteen, still not yet old enough to enter the club as a patron, I was on stage performing a routine I had developed to a track from the *Purple Rain* soundtrack, "Computer Blue."

The transition was far easier than I had anticipated. It helped that Bedroxx was a small hole-in-the-wall type venue. It helped even more that many of the patrons in that small venue happened to be my "friends." The way I saw it, I was just performing for my friends a routine I had already performed countless times behind closed doors. A lap dance was one of the few things I could offer in exchange for the kindness they had shown me, so that's what they received. The story went on that way for a couple of months until my perseverance finally paid off and my life as a club dancer slowly began to fade into black.

Act 3

"So is it true that you're getting married?" came a soft voice from over my left shoulder as I stood in line at the supermarket. I hadn't been at the club for a few months, but it was a voice I instantly recognized. Emily was a flight attendant in her late 20s—a good friend who had been particularly kind to me at a time when I didn't even have a couch to sleep on.

I turned around to find a sort of incredulous look on Emily's face— eyebrows raised in what seemed to be a mocking expression. Ignoring her facial expression, I simply smiled and said yes.

"You're too young!"

At 19 years old I was young, but my decision to get married was one of the few things in my life I felt absolutely certain about. How did I feel?

I had enrolled in community college barely three months after I had walked across my high school graduation stage and collected my diploma. By day, I was working whatever jobs I could around my class schedule, including a student position on campus. By night, the extra money I earned as a stripper allowed me the funds to finally get my first apartment in San Rafael's canal district.

My student gig at the college had eventually transitioned into a full-time classified position with benefits and a salary of $1,800 month. I felt like I had won the lottery. Working on campus while attending classes turned out to be an ideal situation to accomplish what no one else in my immediate family had even attempted: to graduate from college with a four-year degree. On campus, I had also quickly grown an attraction to a beautiful young woman who worked in the cafeteria. This was a community college, though. I was surrounded by beautiful young women, but this was different. There was something about her that immediately fueled a strong attraction. It turns out, when I looked at her, I saw more than a pretty face. In her I saw a chance for something I desperately wanted—a real relationship with someone my own age. I had never had that before. I had had one girlfriend in high school when I was a freshman, but she had been a senior. After she graduated, we continued to see each other off and on, but she was the only high school-aged person I had ever dated. In the young woman in the cafeteria—my future wife—I saw a chance at what I saw as a normal life. As a friend, I was sure Emily would understand that.

"Natalie and I are gonna hang out at my place after the AA meeting. Would you like to join us?" Emily once again raised her eyebrows slightly but this time with a more suggestive expression.

This was the first time my loyalty had been tested. For me, loyalty in part meant always being available. Emily had been good to me, and I had never said no to her before. I wanted something different now, though.

"I don't think it would be a good idea."

I paid for my groceries (ALL of them this time) and we exchanged a somewhat awkward goodbye. That was the last time I ever saw her. I was also leaving behind a way of life. My awkward goodbye with Emily was a point of no return. I could never go back to my life as a dancer. Within a year, my son was born. Two months later at the age of twenty, I married my first wife. There was no Plan B. I had to make this work.

So this unlikely story of a stripper-turned-college professor is going to be a challenging one to cut. If the reader wants to delete the X-rated scenes, well and good, but without them the rest of the story could never happen. That part of the story is full of people who cared for me—maybe not in the most healthy way but in the best way that they could. Maybe my short career dancing at Bedroxx makes for an awkward pitch for the type of movie most studios would want to market, but it was also my escape hatch and the reason that I am here to tell the rest of the story. Bearing all of that in mind, I leave it to the reader to decide what rating this movie shall receive.

Aside from being the mother of an amazingly charming and witty son, **Sartteka am ab Nefer** is a self-defined Black feminist/activist/pedagogue. Tteka is an alumnus of San Diego State University where they received their BA in psychology with minors in both women's studies & LGBT studies, and their MA in women studies. During their academic studies, Tteka was a McNair Scholar and held internships with San Diego Family Justice Center, License to Freedom, Colorado Coalition Against Sexual Assault, Gender Identity Center of Colorado, and San Diego Pride Center. Outside of academia, Tteka is actively involved in their community garden and with political education at Pillars of the Community. Additionally, Sartteka is one of the founding members of BFAB (Black Female Advisory Board). Tteka is a Ra Sekhi Kemetic Reiki practitioner, Kemetic Yoga practitioner, and owner of Asha Nia, a spiritually-guided, (w)holistic healing practice. Their vision is to acquire enough land to farm and live sustainably and to provide fresh healthy produce to others and, ancestors willing, to have many, many, more children. When they are not teaching, growing Asha Nia, fighting white supremacy, patriarchy and the -isms, or volunteering in the community, Sartteka loves to read, write, and enjoy the outdoors.

Sartteka am ab Nefer

Nia

I would like to dedicate this story to the one I lost, the one I let go, and the one that changed my world for the better.

My spirit worked hard to get here. Doctors told my mother that she could no longer become pregnant. They also told her that she had an intrauterine tumor that needed to be removed. However, this tumor turned out to have a heartbeat. Needless to say, I lived. Three years later I was nearly killed in a hit-and-run accident. Doctors were shocked that the impact alone did not cause more physiological damage after I flew 40 feet. Minor scrapes, one broken leg and a fractured skull, but I was alive. Even still, some years later after my suicide attempt, paramedics couldn't figure out how I had consumed between 60 and 75 Celexa with a bottle of Remy Martin at such a young age and didn't die as they forced charcoal into my stomach. I tell you this so that you know, I am here for a reason, and I cannot deny my Nia—my life's purpose.

I experienced my first miscarriage in high school. After that I didn't become pregnant again until meeting my son's dad. In September 2007 I found out I was pregnant again, and I was so happy. Finally, I would have another shot, but in October after being in pain for a couple of days and sick, I went to the emergency room, and doctors were able to confirm that my HCG levels were steadily dropping; they said my baby would pass on its own and within a few days I would start bleeding. It took me awhile to work up the gumption to call home for someone to pick me up because I felt broken, and no matter what anyone said to me I knew it was somehow my fault, something I had done, or something I did not do. Or was it karma? Did I do something so evil in a past life that it left me in debt? Was the universe punishing me? I had no way of knowing for sure, but my suspicion was enough for me and I wanted to give up on life completely, but that was futile. It was just so confusing that the universe would be so cruel as to keep me here in this life without having a child of my own.

Somewhere along the way, the narrative around women and pregnancy has shifted. They say, finish your education first, travel first, settle into your career first, enjoy life first! And we have openly embraced this as a way for women to "put themselves first." But this narrative did not belong to me. Motherhood was what I wanted, and becoming a mother was choosing what mattered most to me and not what the world thought was proper or acceptable. My womanhood was attached to being a mother, and I wasn't going to apologize for it. My identity was entrenched in the indescribable yearning for motherhood. That powerful flame deep in the depths of my soul was my purpose.

A doctor in the ER told me before I left that if I really wanted to get pregnant to just try again. He explained that after pregnancy, whether miscarriage, abortion or delivery, the hormones are still high so the chances of becoming pregnant again are higher—a couple of months later I was pregnant with my son, Kalieaf. I was told to take it easy, but for someone living in my reality that was impossible. I still had to hustle because financially I had no support, and should my baby make it this time I would need to have my shit together. I was the happiest pregnant person ever, and although I had communicated my wish to have a natural birthing experience, Kalieaf was born July 28, 2008 after being induced, so my son's arrival was not the natural birthing experience I had wanted so badly. All of the expectations and ideas I had conjured about what it would be like to bring life into this world were dispelled, but I still felt extremely blessed to have a son, his father's and my first. He was everything. I lay awake just staring at him, crying as he eviscerated my nipples, bearing the pain as I whispered to him that he had saved my life, that there would be nothing I wouldn't do for him and that he was the Nia I had been searching for.

A few weeks before Kalieaf's first birthday party, I found out I was pregnant again and was overjoyed with the thought of finally having the daughter I had always wanted, but I was also terrified. Sometimes our dreams are limited by what's actually happening in real life. This was the case with me. I knew in my heart what my Nia or purpose was, but life's circumstances carved out a very different reality for me. Although I had a close and supportive family, everyone had kids of their own to support, a life of their own, and I was financially doing it on my own. I had gone back to college to try to get out of hustling, but I could not afford to live off the financial aid alone, so I supplemented. Grinding, I took classes and worked my square campus jobs Mondays, Tuesdays and Wednesdays so I could have Thursday through Sunday to trap. I had taken a part-time job on campus tutoring for my psychology professor, which kept me going at times. Going to school full-time, working two student jobs, hustling late nights and early mornings, and still coming home to be a mother to an infant who cried to be fed so often, I had to switch him to formula because I could not pump enough. I was exhausted, my drive was low and I felt that a second child would not improve the static my son's father and I already had due to financial responsibilities. The thought of having a baby on each hip, both potty-training at the same time seemed difficult, being that I had not even been able to get out of the game, which itself required a lot of time and availability. So I let fear creep into my heart distracting me from my life's purpose. I made the decision to have an abortion. I asked my mommy to take me as she has always been my rock, my support, regardless of my decision. I could not sleep the night before; I stayed awake and wrote a poem for my baby. I cried quietly the entire way, in the waiting room, throughout the process and afterward, and the only thing I could tell myself was that I was making this choice for my son so I wouldn't have to take from him before I had enough for them both. I regretted it but told myself that the opportunity would come again someday. I convinced myself to grind harder than before to try to give my son everything and to try to build for us the type of stability that would ensure I would never have to second-guess a blessing should I ever be blessed again.

Since then I've tried repeatedly to conceive: monitoring mucus, temperature, timing. I even asked my primary care physician if there could be something wrong with me. I expressed my fear that something went wrong during my abortion procedure, but he reassured me that nothing was wrong and advised me to lose a few pounds. As we near Kalieaf's ninth birthday I feel less optimistic. Each time someone I know gets pregnant, I fight to keep from breaking down in front of them as I give my support. People tell me maybe it just isn't "the right time," it will happen when it's meant to happen, get your temple healthier.... I have heard it all, and I have tried to see the good intentions in these words of encouragement. Yet all I hear is: time will never be right for you again, you had your shot, it's not him it's you, it's not meant for you, you gave your blessing away and now your ungrateful ass will know the feeling of loss tenfold.

I still feel a crushing pain in my heart at the sight of infants and children. I still cry now but only when I'm alone, so people can't hear me or see me. I try not to share intimate energy with people, as I feel it reminds me that my body can be used in the most temporary sense of the word, that it cannot be purposeful because since my body is broken, my heart is broken. But now I am working to shift my yearning to loving my community because I know that I exist for a purpose beyond myself. And in a way, this is all still mothering. Loving others and loving my son, raising him to be the best young man he can be, and giving him everything just as he has given me. This is still my Nia.

◆ ◆ ◆

Reproductive Freedom: The right to choose if and when to have children. This means honoring women who do not want to have children at all and women who choose not to have children at a specific point in their life. This requires making accessible safe and affordable contraceptives, and, should pregnancy occur, access to safe and legal abortions. In addition, to honor the women who choose to have their children, this requires their right to quality reproductive healthcare by compassionate, culturally competent providers and access to educational material, upholding the women's right to parent their own children and to raise and educate them according to their language, culture, and religion. Reproductive freedom requires that women be protected from taking contraceptives, having abortions and sterilization procedures by force or under duress. For more information about reproductive justice, please visit SisterSong.net.

additional resources

Related Books, Articles, and Films

Mass Incarceration, Criminal Justice, Gang Documentation

- Michelle Alexander, "The New Jim Crow: How the War on Drugs Gave Birth to a Permanent American Undercaste." *The Nation*, March 9, 2010. http://www.thenation.com/article/new-jim-crow/.

- Michelle Alexander, *The New Jim Crow*. This book asserts with extensive documentation that mass incarceration constitutes a new system of racial oppression similar to slavery.

- Angela Davis, "Masked Racism: Reflections on the Prison Industrial Complex." In *Colorlines*, September 10, 1998. In this article, Davis provides a succinct analysis of the evolution of US prisons to being for-profit businesses in themselves that in turn often force inmates to work for other private industries for little or nothing—a modern day slavery.

- *The Atlantic, Angola for Life*, a short 14-minute film produced by *The Atlantic* on the topic of prison slavery. http://www.theatlantic.com/business/archive/2015/09/prison-labor-in-america/406177/. The review and summary of the film is found on this link as well.

- Manny Marable, *Racializing Justice, Disenfranchising Lives: The Racism, Criminal Justice, and Law Reader.*

- City of San Diego, "Frequently Asked Questions Regarding Identifying Gangs and Gang Members." https://www.sandiego.gov/sites/default/files/legacy/gangcommission/pdf/sgufaq.pdf.

- *African Elements: Explorations in Black and Africana Studies*, "Guest Lecture: Guilty by Association? Aaron Harvey and Brandon 'Tiny Doo' Duncan Speak at San Diego City College," June 12, 2015. Filmed by Professor Darius Spearman. http:// africanelements.org/guest-lecture-guilty-by-association-aaron-harvey-and-brandon-tiny-doo-duncan-speak-at-san-diego-city-college/.

Drug Addiction and Treatment

- *New York Times* editorial board, "Drug Deaths Reach White America," January 16, 2016. This editorial asserts that a different response to drug addiction is applied when it is recognized that the victims are white. http://www.nytimes.com/2016/01/25/opinion/drug-deaths-reach-white-america.html?_r=0.

- Tim Wise, "White Denial: America's Persistent and Increasingly Dangerous Pastime," November 25, 2015. http://www.timwise.org/2015/11/white-denial-americas-persistent-and-increasingly-dangerous-pastime/. In this article, originally written for CNN, Wise presents a well-documented argument regarding "colorblindness" or the idea that we live in a post-racial society. Wise is also the author of *Between Barack and a Hard Place*, in which he further explains the fallacies of the idea that we live in a post-racial society.

Addictions

- Gabor Maté, "Addictions Originate in Unhappiness—and Compassion Could Be the Cure." *Yes! Magazine*, Summer 2011 issue. This Canadian physician, author of *In the Realm of Hungry Ghosts: Close Encounters with Addiction*, asserts that addiction is not a manifestation of personal weakness but rather a response to childhood suffering and severe life stressors. http://www. yesmagazine.org/issues/beyond-prisons/why-punish-pain.

Childhood Trauma, Neglect

- *American Academy of Experts in Traumatic Stress.* This website provides insights into the psychological effects on the brain due to trauma. This particular link is about the consequences of early childhood trauma. http://www.aaets.org/article196.htm.

Sex Workers

- Sex Workers Project. This group writes: "As the only U.S. organization meeting the needs of both sex workers and trafficking victims, the Sex Workers Project serves a marginalized community that few others reach. We engage in policy and media advocacy, community education and human rights documentation, working to create a world that is safe for sex workers and where human trafficking does not exist." http://sexworkersproject.org/.

Related Topics

- Tavis Smiley, *Covenant with Black America*. Each chapter, written by a different contributor, outlines one key issue and provides a list of resources, suggestions for action, and a checklist for what concerned citizens can do to keep their communities progressing socially, politically, and economically.

- *African Elements: Explorations in Black and Africana Studies*, "Guest Lecture: Elbert 'Big Man' Howard Speaks at San Diego's

Jacobs Center for Neighborhood Innovation" (June 7, 2015), June 15, 2015. Filmed by Professor Darius Spearman. http://africanelements.org/guest-lecture-elbert-big-man-howard-june-7-2015/.

- Darius Spearman on *African Elements: Explorations in Black and Africana Studies*, "The Conservative Era From Reagan to Obama—Introduction," April 7, 2013. http://africanelements.org/episode-14/.

- Barbara Ehrenreich, "It Is Expensive to Be Poor" from the January 13, 2014 edition of *The Atlantic*. http://www.theatlantic.com/business/archive/2014/01/it-is-expensive-to-be-poor/282979/. In addition to documenting how incredibly difficult it is to get ahead if you're poor, Ehrenreich traces the history of blaming the poor for being lazy, shiftless, and irresponsible, and therefore responsible for their own situation.

Gangs

- Patrick Regan, "Causes of Gang Violence Cannot Be Solved by Enforcement Alone." *The Guardian*, October 27, 2012. http://www.theguardian.com/commentisfree/2012/oct/28/causes-gang-violence-complex-enforcement.

- Shane Liddick in *San Diego City Beat*, August, 2004. Part I: "Gangland San Diego: Gang Activity in America's Finest City," http://sdcitybeat.com/article-1888-gang-land-san-diego.html. Part II: "Gangland America: Finding Common Ground Between Street Gangs, Fraternities and Warring Nations," http://sdcitybeat.com/article-1910-GANGLAND-AMERICA.html.

Prison Gangs

- Jeffrey Toobin, "This Is My Jail." *The New Yorker*, April 14, 2014. http://www.newyorker.com/magazine/2014/04/14/this-is-my-jail.

- Graeme Wood, "How Gangs Took Over Prisons." *The Atlantic*, October 2014. http://www.theatlantic.com/magazine/archive/2014/10/how-gangs-took-over-prisons/379330/.

- David Skarbek and Courtney Michaluk, "To End Prison Gangs, It's Time to Break Up the Largest Prisons." *Politico*, May 13, 2015. http://www.politico.com/agenda/story/2015/05/end-prison-gangs-break-largest-prisons-000034.

Immigration

- Nicholas J. Cull and David Carrasco, *Alambrista and the U.S.–Mexico Border: Film, Music, and Stories of Undocumented Immigrants*. 2004.

Journal Questions

1. Describe the role of gangs in your community and your life.

2. Many of the authors share a turning point in their lives. Write about a turning point in your life.

3. Have you or someone you know ever been impacted by the criminal justice system?

4. Explain how your family has influenced your decisions and other aspects of your life.

5. Write about the neighborhood you grew up in and how it has affected your life and decisions.

6. What are some of the positive and/or negative aspects of the neighborhood where you grew up?

7. How would people describe your neighborhood, and would you agree with their descriptions? How does the reality of your neighborhood match or challenge other people's assumptions?

8. What experiences have you had with the police, the border patrol or law enforcement in general?

9. Have you ever experienced the loss of someone close to you? How did that experience impact your life?

10. How has your race and ethnicity impacted your life?

11. How has your appearance affected your life or how people treat you?

12. Write about speaking a language other than standard English at home.

13. Have you ever been responsible to translate or interpret for a family member?

14. In what ways has immigration impacted your family or community?

15. Write about how a border has impacted your life. This could be a physical, symbolic, or metaphorical border.

16. Do you have a specific story about crossing a border?

17. In what ways are you privileged or not privileged?

18. Have you or someone you know ever been in a toxic relationship? What lessons can be learned from this experience?

19. Write about some of the assumptions people make about you based on your race, religion, sexuality, gender, etcetera.

20. Have you ever made assumptions about a group of people based on an experience that you have had? What are your assumptions about groups of people based on?

21. Write about an educational experience that turned your life around for better or for worse.

22. Many of the stories in this book end in change. Describe the aspects of your life that you would like to change or cultivate.

23. Many of these stories confront traumatic experiences. Write about how you or anyone you have known has experienced something similar.

24. Have you or has anyone you know dealt with serious mental or physical health challenges? Explain the situation.

25. If you could identify one person that you know to read one story in this book, who would it be and which story would it be? Explain the reasons for your choices.

26. If you could interview one of the authors, who would you pick? What would you ask, and how do you think they would answer?

27. Describe your experience—or that of someone you know—with homelessness. Or what is your reaction when you walk past a homeless person or someone begging?

28. Have you ever experienced food and/or housing insecurity?

29. Have you or someone you know been funneled into a bureaucracy?

30. Imagine that you are an author for this anthology. Write your story.

Discussion Questions

1. How do these stories illustrate the resilience and strength of the author(s)?

2. How have the stories in this book impacted you? How do stories help us learn about the world? Consider the role of stories in education and in influencing our understanding of the world.

3. Write a letter to a local lawmaker in which you tell that person your concerns about a situation that comes up in these stories with your recommendations of what needs to be done to improve this situation to give those impacted opportunities to thrive.

4. It has been said that those who are in prison are not the only ones who serve time, but the families also serve time. How do these stories illustrate that?

5. Based on these stories, what does the carceral system currently look like? What should it look like?